"Poignant. Powerful. Achingly real. *Twice-Rescued Child* is a portrait of suffering and surrender that beckons the reader to examine his or her heart, and ask: 'Where is God in the midst of darkness?' From escaping the reach of Hitler's death camps and surviving the depths of grief and loss in a post-war world, to a fully surrendered life in worldwide missions, Thomas Graumann recounts his life experiences with authenticity, wisdom, and uncommon depth. Holocaust historians will find value in the journey, as will those contemplating the call to ministry— anyone ready to share the gospel of Jesus Christ with a broken world."
Kristy Cambron, bestselling author of *The Butterfly and the Violin* and the Lost Castles series

"Open the pages of the *Twice-Rescued Child* and you will be swept into an intimate, first-person account of a Czech Jew who was rescued via the Kindertransport during the early days of the Second World War. His story is told in a way that feels like you're sharing coffee with him, hunched over a small table; you will see the war through a child's eyes, feel his confusion and experience each emotion with him. It's a simple story of a complex time that demonstrates the miracle of being rescued not just once but twice."
Cara Putman, ECPA bestselling and award-winning author of *Shadowed by Grace* and *Imperfect Justice*

"Moving and inspiring! *Twice-Rescued Child* shows how one person's actions can ripple through time. Rescued from the Holocaust by the principled courage of one man and the sacrificial love of his mother, Thomas Graumann was again rescued through faith in Christ—and dedicated his life to missions. Tricia Goyer recounts the amazing life of this incredible man. Not to be missed!"
Sarah Sundin, bestselling and award-winning author of *The Sea Before Us* and *The Sky Above Us*

TWICE RESCUED CHILD

The boy who fled the Nazis and
found his life's purpose

Tricia Goyer is the author of more than 70 books. She writes both fiction and nonfiction related to family and parenting. A *USA Today* bestselling author, she has also won two Carol Awards and a Retailer's Best Award. She was an ECPA Gold Medallion nominee and a Christy Award nominee, and won Writer of the Year from the Mount Hermon Christian Writers Conference.

Tricia is also a beloved author of Amish fiction, having written the Big Sky and Seven Brides for Seven Bachelors series. She has spoken at events such as MomCon, Raising Generations, and Teach Them Diligently conferences, and is host of the podcast *Walk It Out*.

A homeschooling mom of ten, including seven by adoption, Tricia is also a grandmother and a wife to John. With a busy life, she understands the importance of making every word count. You can find out more about Tricia at www.TriciaGoyer.com

TWICE RESCUED CHILD

The boy who fled the Nazis and
found his life's purpose

THOMAS GRAUMANN
WITH TRICIA GOYER

First published in Great Britain in 2019

Society for Promoting Christian Knowledge
36 Causton Street
London SW1P 4ST
www.spck.org.uk

Published in association with Books & Such Literary Management, 52 Mission Circle, Suite
122, PMB 170, Santa Rosa, CA 95409-5370, www.booksandsuch.com

British Library Cataloguing-in-Publication Data
A catalogue record for this book is available from the British Library

ISBN 978–0–281–08312–1
eBook ISBN 978–0–281–08314–5

1 3 5 7 9 10 8 6 4 2

Typeset by Manila Typesetting Company
Printed in Great Britain by Jellyfish Print Solutions

eBook by Manila Typesetting Company

Produced on paper from sustainable forests

I am writing this story at the request of my son Paul and many other friends and family members. This story is for my children and future generations already growing and thriving:

Timothy Andrew Graumann

Lynette and Alan Rice and their three daughters:
Jessica (and Jacob with their son Josiah and an expected addition)
Carissa (and Conner with their daughter Riley)
Amanda

Dan and Wendy Graumann and their four daughters:
Ashley
Brooke (and Jacob)
Cassie
Danyelle

Paul and Melissa Graumann and their three children:
Caela
Trent
Emily

In memory of Františka Hochbergová from Těšany, born July 15, 1910, who displayed great faith in her will for my life, which God fulfilled without her finances or influence,

and

Antonín Graumann from Těšany, born June 21, 1934, my often sickly younger brother and playmate, deported to Terezin on April 4, 1942, and then to Sosibór, Osowa, on May 9, 1942

Contents

Note to the reader   xiii

Introduction   xv

1   Czechoslovakia: August 1939   1
2   Scotland: August 1939   16
3   My second rescue: 1940   24
4   After the Second World War: 1945–1948   35
5   Preparing to be a missionary: 1948–1953   40
6   Glasgow and Liverpool: 1954   50
7   Central Language School: 1955   58
8   Mindoro: 1957   65
9   Villages of the rainforest: 1959–1961   73
10   Caroline: 1961   84
11   A promise of a family: 1962–1966   89
12   Welcoming children: 1966–1967   99
13   Home: 1970–1976   107
14   A visit to the Philippines and Australia: 1990   117
15   A letter from Cousin Honza: 1990–1993   122
16   Education for Democracy: 1993–1994   133
17   Teaching English: 1994–2003   139
18   Nicholas Winton and the power of good: 1997–2002   147
19   EXIT Tour: 2008–2009   152
20   Winton Children: 2014–2016   159

Epilogue: 2016–2018   163

Notes from Tricia Goyer and Paul Graumann   165

Note to the reader

Several terms used by Thomas Graumann in his narrative, such as "tribe(s)," "tribal," "native," "primitive," and "jungle(s)," were in common use in the decades covered in this book but are held by some today to be pejorative. Wherever possible, such terms have been replaced with synonyms.

Introduction

More than six million Jews were systematically annihilated in the Holocaust. It's a number that is hard for us to wrap our minds around. Nearly 80 years after the Second World War, horror and sorrow grip our hearts. We have heard stories of families torn apart, mass graves, and ash from the chimneys that fell like snow. Yet so many individual lives, individual stories, are lost in the pages of time.

Of the six million Jewish people killed during the war, 1.2 million were Jewish children. Little ones who ran barefoot through summer grass, laughed, and played during school recess, and snuggled next to fathers and mothers, listening to stories. At the start of the war, as Hitler's troops invaded country after country, few guessed the heartache to come. Even fewer guessed what was in store for the children. Yet some did, and a few stepped forward to help.

For 669 children, one man's foresight and quick action made all the difference. Nicholas Winton—subsequently Sir Nicholas Winton—an English stockbroker, heard about the plight of Czech children trapped behind the border and in need of sponsors and transportation to the UK. Preparing for a ski trip, he instead traveled to Prague at the request of a friend. Once there, Nicholas recognized the advancing danger. At the time, Hitler's troops had already occupied the Sudetenland, and the German leader had his sights set on all of Czechoslovakia. What would happen to the Jewish children caught up in Hitler's grasp? Stories and rumors were already leaking out concerning the treatment of Jews in Germany and annexed Austria. Discovering children in need of rescue, Nicholas Winton took quick action. Boys and girls condemned to die found life, found families, and some also found saving grace along the way. Today, there are more than 5,000 descendants of these rescued children around the world. This is one child's—one man's—story.

1

Czechoslovakia
August 1939

A gentle stirring on my shoulder pulled me from my sleep. I yawned and opened my eyes, suddenly aware of what day it was. I believed it was going to be a day of adventure. Only years later would I understand it was the day I was snatched from the jaws of death. My first rescue as a child.

At eight years old, I would be riding on a train today, leaving Czechoslovakia behind and traveling to the UK. I sat bolt upright and noticed my mother's still presence as she stood next to my bed.

"Tomík, it's time to wake up." She bent over me and put a finger to her lips. "Shh, you must be quiet though. We don't want them to hear you."

Them meant the Nazi soldiers who were living in our home. Just five months earlier the Germans had invaded our country. It started with Hitler's invasion of the Sudetenland, and now the whole country was in the German Führer's grasp.

For so much of my life I had felt safe and comfortable. During my early years, my parents, brother and I lived with my parents and grandmother in her fine home in Brno, cared for by staff. And after my mother remarried, my mother and stepfather moved us to Těšany where they were managers of an expansive estate. We lived in the *zamek*, or mansion house, and almost everyone in the village worked for my parents. Cooks prepared meals according to Mother's orders. Other hired helpers assisted as needed.

But now, as I walked through the dim rooms with my mother, I was leaving everything behind for a few months . . . or so I thought.

Mother and I walked down the stairs to the front door, which opened onto a large passageway to the courtyard. We passed the kitchen and everyday dining room. The formal dining room was upstairs, connected to the kitchen by a dumb waiter. These rooms were quiet, empty.

As we passed by the children's room, full of toys, I thought of my five-year-old brother Tony, still asleep. He was supposed to be on this train ride too, but he was ill. Tony had had problems with his eyes all his life, and he was often sick. Mother told me that Tony would come on the next train and join me. I liked the idea that my brother would be with me in England soon. His favorite place to play was the sandbox. Maybe there would be one where I was going. We could have quite an adventure together.

Since it was the growing season, agricultural equipment was parked inside the courtyard. In the distance, the barn stalls were filled with 80 cows. The faintest of lowing could be heard in the early morning. The air smelled of fresh earth and growing plants. After a hailstorm just months before, new green leaves were starting to poke up from the ground. Behind the fields, in the property's cottages, lived the harvesters—the farm workers and their families. I was friends with many of those children. What would they say when I didn't come to play with them? Would they wonder where I had gone? Would they be jealous of my great adventure?

My eyes moved to the other side of the courtyard and the blacksmith's shop, where our driver, Karel Ardyl, also worked as a blacksmith and drove a tractor for harvesting. Of course Karel wasn't there today. Instead he stood by the waiting car in his chauffeur uniform. He would be driving Mother and me to the train station in Brno, where Grandmother Helen Hochberg would meet us, and together we would catch a train to Prague.

I settled into the back seat of the automobile next to my mother. She was dressed in a fine dress and hat as usual. Mother always looked her best wherever she went.

"You'll go to England for two months," Mom had told me as we had prepared and packed. "And when Hitler leaves you can return home, and we'll all be together again." Everything had to be done in secret though. The Germans could not find out that I would be leaving or where I was to go.

All the preparation of the last week had led to this moment as we drove away. In the previous days a seamstress had come to the house for a few days to make me new clothes. She came every year to make new outfits for us, but this was different. She worked almost around the clock, preparing for my trip.

Just yesterday, I had been to say goodbye to my birth father. Our chauffeur, Karel, took me to Brno, parked the car, and took me for a long walk to my father's shoe shop. Ever since Mom and Dad divorced and Mom married her second husband, Julius Hochberg, we were not supposed to have any contact with Dad. Every year he made me a pair of boots with his company name on the back, which was dutifully cut off before the gift went under the Christmas tree. Yet now, I had spent the whole day with him at his work, neither of us speaking of the reason I was there.

The shoe shop that he owned was filled with German soldiers. They milled around the room, talking to one another and waiting to be served. Both excitement and fear filled me at their presence. They were foreign and dangerous, and because of their occupation everything had changed within the shop, within our village, within our home.

In the shoe shop, the statue to President Masaryk was covered up so as not to offend the uniformed men. They were buying boots, because my father's boots fit their feet better and were considerably more comfortable than those issued by the German army. The soldiers did not yet know that my father was a Jew. I doubt they would have given him such business if they had guessed.

When my father finally closed his shop for the evening, he took me to dinner. My uncle joined us. My father was living with my uncle's family during that time. Sadness filled his face as we said our goodbyes.

The train ride from Brno to Prague seemed to last forever, and as the train neared Wilson Station the evidences of the Nazis in Prague were clear. We exited the train, and I walked between my mother and grand-mother, holding their hands, my eyes wide.

German soldiers rumbled by on motorbikes. Wehrmacht trucks clogged the streets. As we strode up to Nerudova Street toward Prague Castle, I noticed that the beautiful banners that used to decorate the street leading up to the castle had been replaced with Nazi flags.

I peered up at the fortress on the hill, guessing it had stood for a thousand years, but now it was under German rule. Instead of the

Czech castle guards with their sharp blue uniforms, Germans in brown marched in step as they circled the gates.

From the courtyard of the castle, my mother, grandmother and I viewed Prague. Once the center of the Austro-Hungarian Empire, the fine city spread out before us. As a child, I took no note of the gilded cupolas, baroque towers and tall, pointed spires. It was familiar to me. I knew no other world. It was only years later, after my home country was just a distant memory, that I remembered with fondness the beautiful places of my childhood.

After visiting the castle, we strolled down the cobblestone streets to the Charles Bridge—the most famous bridge in our country—lined with stone statues depicting Catholic saints. I had learned Catholic prayers at school, but at the time they were only words, just like the math formulas and historical dates I had memorized.

We walked across the stone bridge, surrounded by other people, watching important German vehicles rumble past among the animal carts and city buses. Pedestrians filled every free space. Below the bridge, the Vltava River flowed in a gentle manner. White birds—ducks and swans—swam peacefully on its surface. The sky was a brilliant blue, and there seemed to be no cause for worry. Instead, excitement and eager energy pulsated through my chest.

With the warmth of the sun, this day was quite different from the day the Nazis had first taken complete control of Czechoslovakia. On March 15, 1939—less than five months prior—snow lay thick on the ground. Harsh winds rapped against my bedroom window, and gray skies stretched as far as my eye could see. The somber mood of the weather fit the gloom that descended over our country.

From the moment I woke that day, my mother and stepfather had sat near the radio with stricken looks on their faces. It had happened. The Germans had fully occupied our country. I did not understand all the things that my mother and stepfather talked about, but I do remember the warnings of family members from Austria who had urged us to leave the country when we had the chance. It was a warning that wasn't heeded. As secular Jews, we felt very "Czech" (even though we often spoke German), and my stepfather had thought it important that we did not abandon our country in its time of great need.

4

The determination in my stepfather's eyes faded to fear after the occupation. The radio news reported Hitler's tanks driving down Wenceslas Square in Prague, and Hitler himself made a triumphant entry, stepping onto the castle grounds to claim it as his own.

Yet in Těšany, we had been dealing with the Nazis even before that, when the Sudetenland was handed over to Germany. This part of Czechoslovakia was home to three million Sudeten Germans, and the Czechs who lived within those borders had no way to protest. In October 1, 1938, the Nazi army crossed the borders, taking control of this large swath of land.

Just a day later, German tanks rolled into our village. My friend and I had been both scared and excited as we spotted the first tank, but soon the Germans were knocking on the door of my family's house. The soldiers came next, filling every space in our home. Fearful to be noticed by them, Tony and I kept our distance, yet often I would listen to their German words, for unlike most Czechs, our family spoke German in the house and Czech outside our home, since our family was originally from Vienna.

I again listened to their words now as we walked around the streets of Prague.

"Halt!" they cried as they stopped pedestrians and grilled them for information, checking their papers. And "Heil Hitler!" when they passed one another—or pro-German citizens—on the street.

I lowered my head, clung more tightly to my mother and grandmother's hands, and continued walking. Most important for any Jew was to not draw attention to oneself, not to be seen, not to be heard.

We went to Old Town Square next, and waited until the clock struck the hour and the "disciples" emerged from within the elaborate machinery, traveling by twos in an arc around the clock face. This clock had been keeping time for hundreds of years, but would it remember this hour as I would? To the clock it was just another day, but not to me.

To the side of the clock a skeleton, representing the angel of death, rang his bell as the disciples returned inside. Was the chime a warning to all the Jews of my country? A counting-down of hours for the hundreds of thousands of men, women and children who would all be wiped off the face of the earth in the course of the next five years?

In the afternoon we checked into a hotel because my mother wanted me to have a nap, but I was too excited to sleep. In the evening, Mother and Grandmother took me to the Wilson train station. On the platform there was a big table. A kind-faced woman offered me travel papers and a big label, showing the number 652. The label was hung around my neck, and I was told to keep it on for the ride.

When I saw the name on my travel document—Thomas Hochberg—I was upset. I had never used the name Hochberg. Julius Hochberg, my stepfather, had never legally adopted me. In red pencil, my name was changed back to "Thomas Herman Graumann," which is the name on my original birth certificate. Other children filled the platform, and most seemed as excited as I. Everyone else had been leaving recently, and now I got to do the same. My cousins had left for Australia; my uncle Beda was in London with the Czech government. I had heard of cowboys and Indians, and somehow expected them where I was going.

This would be like my visits with my cousins Petr and Ivan, or visits with Grandpa Hochberg at the village near Kromeriz. Or even the visits to the High Tatra Mountains with our Slovak nanny. After staying with different relatives for some days, I always returned home.

Yet, seeing the German soldiers near the train, my mother and grandmother kept their distance. Fear was clear on their faces.

As we prepared to part, Mother leaned down and looked me in the eyes.

"Go and learn English," she said. "If you know English when you grow up, maybe you can represent your father's shoe company in London."

I nodded. This seemed like a good plan to me.

She added, with a smile, "In two or three months Hitler will be gone and you can come home."

Before I boarded the train I gave my mother and grandmother a quick goodbye kiss. Then I eagerly climbed on, carrying my two suitcases filled with new clothes, and a backpack full of food to eat along the way. I don't remember tears on my mother's face, but I have no doubt they soon came, pouring down her cheeks as she watched the train pull away.

The train chugged through Germany and the Netherlands, and it was dark when we reached the end of the line at the Hook of Holland. From there, we had to get out of the train and board a ferry. On the other side of the crossing, the English side, we were directed to a huge warehouse. Here all the children would be divided into groups and sent to the various families who had promised to care for them.

As I took my first breath of English air, I was totally unaware that the moment in the station in Prague, just the previous day, would be the last time I would see my family. I didn't know then that half a century would pass before I once again stepped onto Czech soil.

Even now, at 88 years old, I struggle, trying to imagine my mother's face and trying to see the love in her eyes that allowed her to send me away. It was indeed love that sent me into the arms of strangers, with hopes of keeping me out of Hitler's grasp. And I also believe that Mother had hopes of sending me into the arms of a loving heavenly Father, too. Someone to protect me, to guide me, when she couldn't.

***

The noise of trains, cargo being loaded and unloaded, and people talking, overwhelmed me as I stood on the train platform, waiting for the next leg of my journey. While all the other children were headed for London, I was not. Another girl from the same train and I had sponsors in Scotland. We would be making the rest of the journey without the other children. We were both given one big coin, and one little coin, which covered the cost of lunch for each of us on the train—wieners with English mustard. Then we were sent in a different direction.

I tried to not let fear creep in as I watched for the right train to board. I pushed thoughts of my mother and my brother from my mind. The first hints of longings for them filled me, but I told myself not to worry. We would soon be together again—reunited once the German threat had left our country.

"Tomík!" A familiar voice called over the din of engines and voices, but hearing it made no sense. It was my name, but surely it wasn't directed at me. I released the handle of my suitcase and turned to the voice. There, taking long strides toward me, was Uncle Beda.

I gasped in surprise, and then remembered he too had been sent to England. Uncle Beda had joined the Czech army, ready to defend our country. Instead, for reasons I didn't fully understand, the Germans took over Czechoslovakia without a fight. Instead of going to the battlefield, my uncle—and the rest of the Czech army—traveled with the Czech government in exile to England.

Had Uncle Beda known I was coming? Or had he just happened to see me standing on the platform? I didn't have time to ask. Instead, he greeted me, said it was good to see me, and then rushed to catch a train in the opposite direction. It seemed like a daydream seeing my uncle there, then gone again. Seeing him made my thoughts turn to my family.

My parents, Francis Graumann (Ferry) and Frances Hochberg (Franzi), were married about a year before my birth, which was on January 28, 1931. My father Ferry was a shoemaker and salesman who made hand-sewn custom shoes and boots, following his father in the shoe business. They had a salesroom in the front of the shop, and behind was a sort of factory. My father cut the leather, and had a whole bunch of people sewing. The business always impressed me.

My mother Frances came from a rich family of farm managers. I was born at my grandmother's house in Brno, at Ugartova 15, Kralove Pole, in the north of the city. I was delivered by a midwife, Maria Horníková, and I lived with my family at my grandmother's house until after my brother Tony was born. Grandpa died nine months after I was born, so I never had any memory of him.

Grandmother's house was large and imposing. We had several servants who cooked our meals and cleaned the house. We also had a gardener who took care of the extensive garden. He and his family lived in a separate house attached to the back of ours. In front of the gardener's house was a water pump. Mother warned us not to drink water from this pump, because it was not safe for drinking. The house had an elevator, which took us up and down the four floors and attic. On the southeast corner of the first floor there was a turret, and inside this, a little circular room.

Across the street, there was a small grocery shop where I remember getting delicious sauerkraut. The road had tramlines, and there was a direct tram to the center of town where my father had his shop and factory only a couple of blocks from the main square.

While my parents were busy with work, Tony and I always had a nanny to take care of us. Occasionally we had a seamstress who came for several days at a time to make us a new set of clothes.

I looked down at the new clothes I was wearing as I waited to board the next train. I remember thinking there was a lot of preparation for a trip that would last just a few months, but I didn't question this. Mother always liked to be prepared.

My father liked to drive fast cars, and according to my cousin, Lisl, Mom encouraged him to drive faster. Dad used his car for business trips and for family outings. We were very close to our relatives, and many of them came to visit us frequently. We often went to the theater as a family, and my mother attended other events as she climbed the Brno social ladder.

On my father's side, my great-grandfather, Joseph Graumann, was born in Osoblaha in Silesia, now North Moravia, in 1830. He was baptized into the Catholic Church, either because of pressure on the family—often called "forced conversion"—or as a means of assimilation into the Czech culture. As a family, the Graumanns worked at textile production and were rich enough to send Joseph to school. He was 18 at the time of the 1848 revolution. At that point all young Czech men were liable to serve for seven years in the Austrian army.

To escape from military service Joseph crossed the mountains on foot, avoiding mountain passes, which would have been guarded. He trekked eastward toward the High Tatra Mountains. On the way he met a Jewish girl, Hanni, in the Turčiany Valley, married her, and settled down near Martin, in Slovakia. They had five children, but only the birthdates of the sons are recorded: Moritz (1849), Johanna, Herman (1854), Pepi, and Jakub (1861).

Hanni died, and Joseph raised the family alone. After the children were grown, he moved to another Slovakian town, married again, and had a second family. His second wife was Jenny from Turciansky Svaty Mikulas. They had two boys and two girls. My grandfather, Herman, was the second son.

Herman went to school at Žilina. When he was 14 years old his father took him to Žilina, gave him one guilder, and sent him down the Vah River to go to Vienna and learn a trade. Herman's older brother Moritz was already in Vienna working as an apprentice to a tailor. His younger brother Jakub followed later to learn ironwork.

My grandfather learned to make shoes, and he also served his compulsory military training at Nitra, in Slovakia, in the famous Austrian

Dragoons. Later, as a master craftsman, he moved with his brother to Brno to set up his business. All of these places were in the Austro-Hungarian Empire at that time.

Grandfather married and had four children. Uncle Arthur (1889) was the firstborn and the only one of his siblings to perform the bar mitzvah ceremony. Later, when Uncle Arthur worked as a lawyer, he found it inconvenient to be a Jew. Uncle Fritz (Fredrich) was born in 1892, then Aunt Ilka in 1895, and Dad in 1898. There were several marriages between the Graumanns and the Flatters—Uncle Arthur, Uncle Fredrich and Uncle Otto.

My father, Ferry Graumann, was a shoemaker and left for work before I was up and came home after I was in bed, so I saw very little of him except at weekends and on family trips, such as ski holidays. When Dad arrived home from business trips, he always brought a gift: several boxes of spa wafers. These were round, sugary Czech wafers, made with special spa water that was supposed to be healthy.

Three years after I was born, in 1934, my brother Tony arrived. When I was about five and Tony about two, we were sent to live with another family for a few months. When we returned we found my parents had divorced and Mother was remarried to Julius Hochberg from the village of Lutopecny, near Kromeriz.

Uncle Beda Hochberg—my stepfather's brother—was married to Hanna, and he had two sons, Petr and Ivan. We often stayed in their home. It was at Uncle Beda's that I first rode in a horse and carriage. Once, I remember Petr found some matches. We started playing with them on the carpet and almost set the house on fire, for which I was spanked and sent to stand in a corner with my face to the wall. When we returned to Brno and Grandma's house, I loved playing horse and carriage with the lawn furniture in the garden.

Not far out of Brno was the farm of the Otto Cantors, cousins on my mother's side of the family. I remember visiting them and sitting in front of a huge fire in the fireplace. There was always a big tureen of delicious home-made soup on the table.

My cousin Lisl had told me that when Uncle Beda had gone to England he had changed his name to Jan Horský. Maybe he thought exchanging his Jewish name for a Czech one would help him get the right documents to bring his family to England to join him. I wasn't sure. I did know that both my own life and Uncle Beda's had already changed so drastically because of the Germans.

All through my growing-up years in Czechoslovakia we always had nannies to look after us. They usually wore a habit and were probably Catholic nuns. None of them stayed with us very long, except Fisher. For several years while we lived in Těšany, we went with Fisher to visit her home in Slovakia. Her house was in a village on the lower slopes of the Tatra Mountains. Neither trains nor buses came to this remote place. When we got to the house the snow was up to the upstairs windows, and a hole had been cut through the snow to allow us to get to the front door. There was no running water in the building. We had to go to the end of the garden and let a bucket down the well to get water. This was a great place to ski.

One day after a long day of skiing, I could not get out of bed. The Fishers loaded me onto a toboggan and took me to a doctor in another village. He prescribed wrapping me in a cold wet sheet. I did not like this treatment, but it apparently cured me.

Looking back, what I remember most is time spent with my nannies. Yet even if I didn't often feel my mother's hugs and embraces—and don't have many memories of kisses and caresses—during my growing-up years in Czechoslovakia my every need was satisfied. I had everything, but my heritage caused me to lose it all. I was a Jew. The label had been a burden for my people for centuries before I was born.

***

As an adult I learned that long before I was born, during my grandfather and great-grandfather's time, the land known as Czechoslovakia was part of the Austro-Hungarian Empire. The Czechs had been the primary inhabitants of Bohemia since the sixth century AD and were joined by German immigrants in the thirteenth century. By 1620 Bohemia had come under the control of the Habsburg monarchy, along with the Archduchy of Austria and the Kingdom of Hungary. Yet the subjected peoples of the Austro-Hungarian Empire wanted to be free from the rule of the imperial family. The empire crumbled during the First World War, and the Czechs and Slovaks were allowed self-rule.

In 1918, after the First World War, new boundaries were formed. Slovakia was joined with the Czech lands because the two regions shared a similar language. This new nation state was bordered by Germany to the west, Austria to the south, and Poland to the northeast. But 20 years after the end of the war there were many who were still unhappy with the new boundaries. Pro-German supporters wanted to be part of Hitler's Germany. Germany also had its eye on the border areas where there was much industry, including companies controlled by Germans and German-owned banks. Industrial resources like iron, and the ability to build secure defenses within these new borders, would help Germany grow in power. Also, as a result of the boundaries designed after the Great War, more than three million Germans found themselves within the Bohemian and Moravian border regions known as the Sudetenland.

Hitler rose to power in Nazi Germany in 1933, and the German annexation (Anschluss) of Austria came in 1938. Once Austria was in his grasp, Hitler's next desire—and indeed demand—was to control the Sudetenland. He threatened to wipe out the Czech nation if he didn't get it, and he promised not to venture onto other Czech lands if the Sudetenland was handed over. On September 29, 1938, the Munich Agreement gave Hitler control of the Sudetenland. This agreement was signed by Germany, Italy, France and the UK; Czech leaders had no part in the talks.

On October 1, our family found itself living within these borders. This was bad enough for our Czech neighbors, but as Jews my family felt even more threatened. All my ancestors on both my mother's and father's side were Jews. Grandmother frequently went to the synagogue and also to the Jewish cemetery to put flowers on the family graves.

Jews have lived almost constantly in the Czech lands. According to the oldest historical records there were always Jewish traders in Prague. Around AD 900, someone wrote that in the marketplace in Prague there were Jews and the market was an excellent place to become rich. Around the year 1000, rabbis who were escaping from the Muslim forces advancing on Jerusalem came to Prague. Over the centuries several of the Prague rabbis became famous, especially Rabbi Loew.

In the early days of the Prague Jewish community, Jews were glad to be assigned a section of the city where they could live in peace. Inside their ghetto they had self-government and practiced Judaism under the leadership of their rabbi. However, especially at Easter time when the story of the crucifixion and resurrection of Jesus was re-enacted elsewhere, the illiterate crowds decided, "The Jews are Christ-killers. Let's kill the Jews."

At Easter time in 1389, members of the Prague clergy accused the Jews of desecrating the eucharistic wafer (the Host). Incensed mobs sacked and burned the Jewish quarter, and killed nearly the entire Jewish population of the city, some 3,000 people.

The Czechs, as good Catholics, did not want to be polluted by mixing with Jews. The Czech kings usually promised the Jewish community protection, for which they had to pay high taxes. Although forbidden to work at many occupations, they were allowed to carry out trading and banking, because the "Christians" felt that handling money was dirty work. Inside the Jewish community they were allowed to butcher their own animals according to their kosher tradition. However, they were forbidden occupations such as building, so their synagogues were built by Christians. When Jews were expelled from Prague in 1542 and 1561, as they were from 80 other European cities, they were soon invited back, because the king needed their services.

***

Things never got easy for the Jews, and when I was a child, what was happening to the Jews in Germany and Austria was well known in Czechoslovakia. Many Jewish families were unsure of what to do—whether they should leave their homeland or stay.

I can't remember the first time I heard about the danger of Hitler's army, but I do remember that people in my family were divided about how German occupation would affect us, our lives, and our futures. Some of my family members believed it would be safe for us to stay—after all, we were Czech. We related more to our Czech heritage than our Jewish one. Yet other relatives sensed the impending doom.

My father Ferry, my uncle Beda—Mother's brother—Aunt Ilka and her husband Edgar Oser all advised staying. But there were other family members who believed that no Jew would be safe in a land under Hitler's control.

Once Hitler took over Austria, 150,000 Jews escaped from Vienna. Among those leaving were Emmanuel and Kamila Mandl, and their daughter Lisl. Kamila was the sister of my stepfather Julius. Every summer they came to Těšany to see us, but in 1938 they came to stay until they acquired a visa to go to either the USA or Australia. They spoke of what they had seen in Vienna—Jewish shops closed up; teachers and doctors not allowed to practice; Jews banned from traveling by tram, bus or train; Jewish children unable to go to school. Would that happen in Czechoslovakia too?

Finally Emmanuel and Kamila Mandl's papers arrived, allowing them to travel to Australia. They even received permission for our family—my mother, stepfather, brother and me—to join them, but in the end my stepfather and mother decided to stay. Life was very comfortable at the mansion in Těšany, and they had no intention of leaving. But shortly afterwards it was too late, even if my family had wanted to go. Our village was part of the Sudetenland, soon under German control.

On October 1, 1938, the first Nazi tank rolled into our village—and ended up in a ditch in front of the mansion. I was walking home with my friends from school, and we stopped to watch the soldiers laboring to get the tank out of the ditch.

From that point on, a Nazi officer stayed in our home and ate meals with us. Sometimes there were more officers, but always at least one. Mother warned Tony and me not to go anywhere near the German soldiers, not even to look at them. We were to be quiet and still in their presence. The more time went on, the more Nazis joined us at our table.

Nazi soldiers also lived in various other houses throughout the village. They traveled up and down the roads in motorcycles with sidecars. The soldiers in the sidecars always carried long poles, and they thought it was great fun to knock people down with their sticks as they drove by.

Around this time, the pastor of the Evangelical church near our village often visited my mother. Jan Odstracil often brought his son Jan, who played with us in the sandbox in the garden. I didn't know what these visits were about. I thought they were about a community need my mother was helping with. She always made sure to give money to the poor and help in any way she could. Even when directing the harvesters,

Mother was very careful to ask them to leave something in the fields for the poor to gather—a very good Old Testament teaching.

Only later did I discover Jan Odstracil's connection with Nicholas Winton, and my mother's plans for my brother and me to travel to the UK, in hopes of finding safety. It was the Evangelical pastor who was the first to step forward to save my life.

Yet when I stepped onto that train, heading for Scotland, I had no idea of all the work that had already been done to protect me, to steal me from the Germans' grasp. As a young boy I was simply curious about who my sponsor would be. Who would be waiting at the train station at the other end? With my mind still on adventure, I looked forward to getting to know the family who would look after me for a time, not understanding that from this moment I would never again be cared for by all those whom I had loved and trusted.

2

Scotland

August 1939

I walked into the large, barn-like room with camp beds in a row down each side. "The boys' dorm," someone had told us. I guessed that the girls also had a dorm similar to this one in another part of the building. The wooden floors were hard and cold, but there were plenty of blankets and pillows. Even though it was August, the damp wind was cool—a noticeable difference from back home.

After seeing Uncle Beda, I had enjoyed an uneventful train ride to Scotland, except for the hot English mustard. I had smeared it generously on my sausage and had taken a bite before I realized it was not the mild mustard from home. The spices bit at my tongue and throat. Tears sprang to my eyes.

We had got off the train at a town called Selkirk. I looked around and noted the two-level houses, separated from one another by a garden. With the other children I walked in line to a large home called "The Priory." Children filled every part of the space, and most seemed to be speaking languages I didn't understand.

As I placed my suitcase near the bed that was pointed out to me, I heard sniffling.

"Mutti, Mutti," a small boy cried in German. He was curled into a tight ball on a bed in the opposite row.

An older boy approached me. "He's crying for his mother," he said, speaking in Czech.

I nodded, understanding.

The boy told me his name and explained that he had been there a while, from a previous transport.

I soon found out that there were many of these older boys, and I looked up to them. They seemed tough, and I wondered if they ever thought about their family back home. Did they see this as an adventure too? Yet instead of acting excited, or even sad, they often behaved in angry ways. They complained about the weather, since it seemed to rain every day. They also complained about the food.

I didn't pay them too much attention. I played on the swings and in the sandbox with the other kids. I discovered we didn't need to understand one another's languages to have fun. On Sunday, we marched to the Church of Scotland parish church. Everything was in English, and I didn't comprehend a thing. Why was I even there? I was just eager to get back and play again.

One day, I heard shouts rising from the dining room. The older boys had scraped the last of the food from their plates and were still hungry.

"Come on, Tommy!" one of the older boys called to me. Excitement filled his gaze, and he turned and rushed toward the kitchen. I got up from the table and followed him. In the kitchen, the older boys were stuffing raw potatoes into their pockets, much to the protest of the kitchen workers.

"Let's go!" another boy called, and ran outside. A trail of boys followed, and I hurried to catch up.

The rowdy group rushed to a spot in the back of the property. Working as a unit, they gathered wood and built a fire. With great excitement they placed the potatoes in the flames, and we chatted while they roasted. It wasn't long before a hot potato was put into my hands. I glanced around to make sure there were no adults coming to find us, and ate it hurriedly.

There were enough potatoes for every boy, but when we were finished we weren't sure what to do. Hoping we wouldn't get into too much trouble, we all hurried back to the Priory, and I rushed to play with my friends. If anyone was ever punished for this act of rebellion, I never heard about it.

Not many weeks later, one of the female workers approached me. "Tommy, we have a home for you."

Without question I followed the woman. My mother and grandmother had always taught me to obey and respect adults.

We traveled to Dunbar, to the home of Pastor Sawyer. The aroma of the salty air in this coastal town enhanced my feelings of being on holiday—so different from home. Boats with tall masts were docked in the calm harbor, looking like large versions of children's toys. Surrounding the harbor, large rocky hills rose from the water, and I imagined climbing them to gain a view of the sea beyond. On one of those hilly areas stood the remnant of a castle.

At this new home, two kids my age were eager to play: John and Claire. The family lived in a big house (called the Manse), belonging to the church, with a large garden and lots of fruit trees. Across the street, on the waterfront, was the town's swimming pool. We spent a lot of time either in the pool or in the garden during those warm summer days. Often, at high tide, the swimming pool was evacuated because the waves broke over the wall of the pool and filled it with cold seawater.

At the end of the garden there was a gate, and across an alley was a door to a little shop. Pastor Sawyer took me to the door of the shop and taught me to say my first English sentence: "Players, please." He was sending me in to buy cigarettes for him.

As I spent time with John and Claire, I began to pick up more words, but even though I didn't understand very many phrases, after two weeks I knew that something was different. The adults had grown serious, anxious, and I soon found out why. Pastor Sawyer had been called up to the army as a chaplain. Since he would no longer be serving as pastor, the family would be losing their home.

An uneasy knot grew in my stomach. John and Claire's father was going into the army. They and their mother would be leaving Dunbar to live with her father in Yarrow, near Selkirk. He was a retired minister who had been asked to take the place of another pastor, who had also been called up into the British Army. Change was happening all around me. My things were again packed into my small suitcase.

I thought back to the home I had just left. The estate in Těšany was about the size of a city block, with ceilings 15 feet high on each floor of the house. The barn itself was three stories high and two city blocks long, with the equipment on the first level, cows on the second floor, and the feed on the third floor so that each day it could be scraped off to the pens below. That old life seemed like a dream. What was happening now to those I had left behind? What awaited me next?

**

Miss Mary Corson had never expected to have to stay in Scotland. She had been a teacher at Tabitha School in Jaffa, Palestine, yet because of the war she hadn't been able to return. The school in Jaffa was run by the Church of Scotland Mission to the Jews, but most of the children attending it were Arabs.

When asked to sponsor children in need, Miss Corson offered to take two girls. Scanning a card with photos of various children, she chose two sisters from Prague. Arrangements were made with the parents, both of whom were pediatricians. But at the last moment they couldn't force themselves to put their girls on the train and send them away. They didn't realize this was their last opportunity to save their lives. The Scottish Trust asked Mary Corson if she would take two boys instead.

Miss Corson paused before giving an answer. "I don't know if I can handle two boys. I'll try it for a month."

So I was put on a train again, this time headed to Connel, on Scotland's west coast. I disembarked and found myself standing with another Czech boy, Tom Schlesinger. Tom and his mother had managed to get out of Czechoslovakia before the Germans had taken control of the country. His father, a lawyer, was unable to leave. His mother worked as a waitress in England but was not making enough money to support them both.

Tom and I noticed a small cluster of people approaching. Miss Corson, her sister, brother-in-law and cousin all met us. Miss Corson shook our hands, and together we walked five minutes to her house.

Miss Corson seemed like a little old lady to me, with her white hair done up in a bun at the back of her head. She was a petite, thin woman and wore simple dresses and sweaters, yet she had a lot of energy. She had studied French, Italian and Spanish, but that was no help to us. She smiled at me, and seemed very welcoming, even if I didn't understand a word other than "yes" and "no," "please" and "thank you." In her home, the table was loaded with good things, and we got to eat whatever we wanted.

Miss Corson's sister was a little older and retired. Her brother-in-law served in the pastorate in the Church of Scotland. They stayed for a week after we arrived, and her cousin Alice stayed a bit longer and visited frequently. Aunt Alice lived in Oxford and had a little bird, Budgy.

Miss Corson had a parrot named Polly, and Tom and I would often take the bird into the garden with Budgy. Miss Corson was a good gardener and we helped her grow a lot of vegetables.

"Tommy," she would call to me, waving me over to help her weed or pick the vegetables.

Only rarely did I think back to my grandmother's garden, which was mostly full of flowers. Or the garden at the mansion, with bigger plots of vegetables and fruit.

Connel, previously called Connel Ferry before the bridge was put in, was becoming my new home. It was a little village with about 200 houses, mostly large, single-family homes with generous gardens. The houses were spread out over a mile or two along the south shore of a narrow lake, Loch Etive. The village had three hotels, two grocery stores, a butcher, a post office, a village hall, two Protestant churches, and a little Catholic church.

Mary Corson was a teacher of home economics. She taught me how to knit, and I still knit socks to keep my feet warm. She taught me to cook, and my grandchildren love the zucchini muffins I bake for them. She read the Bible every day and prayed before meals. In Scotland, the Presbyterians called Sunday "Sabbath" and applied all the Old Testament laws about the Sabbath to Sunday. Food was always prepared the day before. Fires were not lit on Sunday. We walked to a church in the village and did not travel, shop or eat out. Sunday was a day of rest for worship and Bible study. Schoolwork had to be completed on Friday and Saturday.

Soon after our arrival in Connel it became necessary for all foreigners to register with the police, make an annual police report, and get permission to travel before going to a different address. German and Austrian nationals were interned on the Isle of Man. Uncle Otto Flatter was interned there. In 1938 his wife had been invited to be a piano accompanist for a concert in London. When they both arrived in London they requested asylum.

Tom Schlesinger and I settled into a simple routine with Miss Corson, and at the end of the month she reported to the authorities that she was doing all right and would try to keep us for another month. I of course did not know about this arrangement.

The building to the east of Miss Corson's house was the local school, Achaleven Public School. It was a two-roomed building. One room was for the younger children, aged four to six, and the other room was for grades one through five—up to the age of eleven. I was nine years old so participated as much as possible in third grade, and during the course of the year picked up some English, and was able to do the assignments for the class. Between classes we had breaks, during which we played football (soccer) or rounders, which is something like baseball. After school we often played with the other children in the village and probably learned more English through our games than in class.

On the lower ground floor of the village hall were some one-roomed apartments for poorer people. The hall was used for concerts, where different people from the village demonstrated their talents, and also for indoor badminton. On Saturdays, Miss Corson taught a "Band of Hope" children's class there.

On the hillside above the shops was a development of "council houses"—cheaper housing. The rest of the people lived in large detached homes. Tom and I got to know all these houses well, as each Saturday we collected paper and other items "for the war effort" or for recycling. Many of the houses had once had smart iron railings around their front gardens, but these had been removed and claimed by the UK government due to a national shortage of iron. In all the fields, large posts were erected to prevent enemy planes from landing.

This was part of Britain's efforts to fight off an imminent German invasion. Other measures were taken too. Netting was stuck over windows to prevent broken glass from injuring people in the event of a bombing attack. Windows were carefully covered with black fabric at night to block any light that might be a target for enemy pilots. Car lights were dimmed. We were all issued gas masks, and air-raid shelters were constructed. When the south of England was bombed in 1940, many English children were evacuated to the safety of the Scottish mountains.

Throughout the Second World War, Connel had a "Home Guard." This was a local brigade mostly made up of men who were veterans of the First World War. Many of them had been wounded and still carried the scars of that earlier war. As they marched through the village, they carried wooden rifles. We would often join a number of other boys to watch the Home Guard practice. We were there one Sunday afternoon when they were given instruction in the use of a rifle—and had one actual rifle. Each man took a turn to clean, load, and shoot this weapon at a target.

The army brought a unit to the area to construct living accommodation for military families and build a floating dock in a bay near Dunstaffnage Castle, about three miles from Connel. When these soldiers arrived in Connel their commanding officer went from house to house looking for rooms available for army personnel. Four young men stayed with us in one big room, replacing the double bed with two sets of bunk beds. A truck came early every morning, going from house to house, picking up the soldiers. They were taken to work at Dunbeg, the location of the new base, and brought back to sleep at night. From these soldiers I learned how to press army uniforms and polish silver buttons. By the time the naval base was completed, it was bigger than Connel.

When the base was finished, one of the men working on the Dunbeg project, who was newly married, begged Miss Corson to allow him and his wife to lodge at her house. So for about a year a young Christian couple lived with us.

In North Connel, at the opposite end of the bridge across Loch Etive, there was a landing ground for British Spitfires, and the planes frequently flew under this bridge. Close to the north side of the bridge were several houses and a hotel, and one day a German man rented a room in one of these houses. Tom and I visited this man, and Tom noticed that he spoke with a distinct Berlin accent. Because he was living so close to the bridge, Tom and I were suspicious that he was a German spy and was planning to blow it up. We told Miss Corson, but she said this was nonsense. He was just a very nice gentleman. Very soon he was gone and no one knew where he went.

A lady named Helen Forbes lived at the other end of Connel. She was taking care of her aged father. Old Mr Forbes loved ships. He had built his house in a location where he had a good view of his boat, anchored in Loch Etive. Early in the Second World War all possible boats were requisitioned by the UK government for the "war effort." He lost his beloved ship. On Sunday afternoons Tom and I usually went to Helen Forbes' house for "tea." She taught us simple Christian songs known as "choruses," and Bible verses. After her father died, she held Bible studies for military people.

Miss Sturrock, a former missionary to the Congo, stayed with Miss Forbes for a prolonged time. This was my first introduction to foreign missions. With very little training she had gone to the mission field, worked hard, and at an early age returned home sick. She represented the European Christian Mission (ECM), and she gave us some literature published by this organization: a children's magazine edited by Mrs Harris and a correspondence course taught by Mr Stuart Harris, British Director of ECM and formerly a missionary to Czechoslovakia. This course included a study of biblical missionary principles, the history and geography of every country in Europe, and a survey of missionary work in each country.

During the Second World War there was only an occasional bus between Connel and Oban, the main town in the area. If we went to Oban to attend a cinema, we had to walk five miles home after the show. We went very seldom, but there was one film that I never forgot. The story concerned an officer in the Boer War in South Africa. He took his little daughter to a boarding school, where she was very warmly received because her father was an army officer. She had a beautiful room, with lovely clothes, and was well treated. When news reached the school that her father had been killed, the little girl was pulled out of her nice room. Her pretty clothes were taken away and she was given a camp bed in the attic with the servants. Many years later, when I heard that all of my immediate family had died in concentration camps, I remembered this film and wondered what would happen to me. But at the time, before my loss, I settled in as best as I could at my new home, counting the days until I could return to my family.

3

My second rescue
1940

Even though I had hoped to leave the Germans far behind me, it was clear I hadn't gone far enough. Additional siding was laid on the south side of the Connel Bridge train station to support the added wartime traffic. My English was getting better, and I started to understand more of what was happening in the world around me. German bombing started in France, Holland and Belgium early in 1940, and London became a target later in the year. The Blitzkrieg—or "lightning war"—brought massive destruction to the targeted sites. There was an extensive air raid in the Birmingham area, central to England, and a ferocious attack wiped out the town of Clydebank, near Glasgow, just missing the shipyards. This was the only major bombing in Scotland.

We listened to both the BBC and the Nazi propaganda reports on the radio. For each skirmish, the BBC would claim the Allies had won the battle, and then in a German report on the very same battle, the Nazi regime would claim it was the victor.

At the cinema, we saw newsreels of Londoners huddled together in air-raid shelters underground. Some sat nervously while others sang and played accordions. Rationing had begun, and a man by the name of Churchill became prime minister.

As I saw what was happening in the world, I couldn't help but wonder about what was going on at home. But soon the good news of salvation that I received brought hope to my heart, even in troubling times.

To the north of Connel was a town called Benderloch. Mountains rose up not far from the water's edge, and the scent of salty air hung heavy on the breeze. In a small seaside cottage lived a retired couple, who had moved there for the duration of the war. Their one decision—to invite the woman's brother to join them—was to have an impact on my entire life.

Richard Hudson Pope, the brother of Helen Forbes' friend in Benderloch, was an evangelist working with the Children's Special Service Mission (CSSM). The CSSM provided summer children's ministry on the beaches of vacation resorts. Their Scripture Union branch, through its Bible-reading notes, encouraged people around the world to read the same Bible verses day by day. The CSSM also had a ministry in high schools, which included "Inter-School" camps.

Eager to reach the children around Benderloch with the Christian message, Mr Pope started children's meetings in the village hall and the Presbyterian church in May 1940, when I was nine years old. The rooms were full, and I listened intently, attempting to understand his words.

I had already done three years of school back in Těšany, and had completed third grade. On my first day of school, when the Catholic priest arrived to give instructions to my class, my teacher sent me home because she knew my family was Jewish. Mother sent me straight back. She wanted me to get Christian teaching with the rest of my class. We had the same teacher all three years until the Nazis arrived and replaced our teacher with a German-speaking teacher. Even though I was left-handed, I was forced to write with my right hand, which was very difficult, but that was a minor issue compared to the repeated emphasis on Nazi doctrine. Teachers touted the idea that everyone was now united under a strong leader. They spoke of sameness and equality, but as a Jewish boy their words didn't include me.

Several of our nannies took us to church for Sunday mass, unless we had some other, family activity that Sunday. With my class I attended First Communion, but had no idea what I was doing, or what all the crucifixes meant, other than that you had to kiss the feet of the crucifix at the entrance door, but we didn't enter the church there—we came in through the priests' changing room and sat in the choir seats between the altar and the pulpit.

Now, in a different language, in a foreign country far from home, I was to discover what the story behind the crucifix was all about.

***

The tall man stood at the head of the room. "Jesus calls all boys and girls to come to him," Mr Pope declared with enthusiasm. "He promises he will not turn anyone away."

Tom and I listened intently as he explained important Scripture passages. I did not understand every word, but I could understand the meaning. More than that, something in my heart told me that what he said was true.

"Come to me, all you who are weary and burdened, and I will give you rest," he read from Matthew 11.28.

My mind focused on that word *come*. Mr Pope told us that God wanted us near.

"All those the Father gives me will come to me, and whoever comes to me I will never drive away," he explained on another day, reading Jesus' words from John 6.37. Mr Pope explained that we all sin in words, deeds and thoughts because we are sinners, and we cannot go to heaven unless God forgives our sin. And then he shared a verse that filled my heart with joy.

"John 3.16 says, 'God so loved the world that he gave his one and only Son, that whoever believes in him shall not perish but have eternal life.'" Mr Pope scanned the room. "The good news is that Jesus died for our sins. He took our punishment, and because of the sacrifice of Jesus, God offers us the righteousness of Jesus instead of our sins. The apostle John wrote: 'If we confess our sins, God is faithful and just and will forgive our sins.'"

I bowed my head and, using the words of a chorus that Mr Pope had taught us, we sang about Jesus, our Lord, coming into our hearts to stay. Both Tom and I decided to accept Christ. I understood what it meant. I knew I had been given a free gift, one that I could never lose.

Hearing of my decision, Mr Pope approached my desk and handed me a "decision card" with a picture depicting a scene from John Bunyan's *Pilgrim's Progress*. It showed a soldier in armor facing an army under the command of Satan. There was also a place for a signature.

"Do you choose to follow Christ?" asked Mr Pope.

I nodded. "Yes, sir."

A smile lit up his face. "Put down your name, sir."

I signed my name, and I knew things were different now. I was God's child, and I would never be turned away, sent away.

Then Mr Pope leaned over me. "To grow spiritually, you need to read the Bible every day. Here is a Scripture Union card. Each day read these verses, which thousands of people all around the world are reading together."

I started reading the Scripture Union passages daily. I continued this for many years, and later I also answered the suggested questions about the passage. These questions included:

What does this passage teach about God?
What does this passage teach about the Lord Jesus Christ?
What does this passage teach about the Holy Spirit?
Is there an example to follow?
Is there a sin to avoid?
Is there a command to obey?
How does this apply to my life?

The more I read, the more I began to understand what I was reading.

Spring slipped into summer, and Tom and I were invited to the Inter-School Camps (ISC). Most of the boys who attended these camps came from the big secondary schools in which the CSSM had regular classes. Tom and I went there even though we were much younger than most of the high-school campers.

The Scottish boys who attended came from many different schools. During every camp the boys would gather and sing together:

We're all together again, we're here, we're here
We're all together again, we're here, we're here
And who knows when we'll be together again
We're all together again, we're here, we're here.

I continued going to these camps every year through high school. I learned a lot of things about the Christian life, and every year came home with new books. I was introduced to C. S. Lewis's *Screwtape Letters*, and the Weymouth New Testament. I also learned practical things such as how to pitch bell-tents and marquees (tents big enough to hold meetings for a hundred people), dig holes for outhouses, and help in the camp kitchen. There were usually 100–150 kids at each camp, and each tent group was responsible for chores such as washing cooking-pots, cleaning vegetables, and peeling potatoes.

We played special games. Puddox was a game somewhat like cricket or baseball. It was played with a round bat like a baseball bat, but batters stood in front of wickets as in cricket, and ran back and forth between these sticks, 22 yards apart. The other game was rugger and was played rather like touch rugby, but the rules allowed the oval rugby ball to be thrown forward as well as backward.

Yet even though those times were fun, it was the daily devotions in each tent—and the meetings of the whole camp every evening—that I most treasured. They were special spiritual experiences for me. The Bible-based, encouraging and motivating messages renewed my dedication to the Lord. The strong example set by high-school leaders, and the music, made it special. I was reassured by the words of spiritual songs such as:

> Just as I am, young, strong and free,
> To be the best that I can be,
> For truth and righteousness and thee,
> Lord of my life, I come.

Stewart Dinnen, one of the campers, was an excellent musician. He wrote the song:

> Lord of our boyhood days, we call to you,
> Cleanse us from every sin, from guilt set free.
> Lord, make our paths to lie where your feet trod,
> That we may grow in you, strong men of God.

We also had fun singing new songs written by campers, such as:

> Good food for fellows in their teens
> Tomato soup and lots of greasy beans
> And a ladle full of porridge in the morning.

> Good tents in which we sleep and snore
> Too bad if you lie near the door
> Good food, they'd lick it off the floor
> And a ladle full of porridge in the morning.

Yet summer camps weren't all fun. The summer holidays were short, as there was another holiday later in the year for picking potatoes. Many of the ISC camps were working camps. We picked raspberries for a jam factory in Perthshire, and potatoes in Ayrshire.

***

As time passed, I knew that it would most likely be years—not months—until I saw my family again. From the time I left, Mother had kept in touch. She would write very short notes. They arrived every week at first, and the notes said basically the same thing: "We are doing fine, Tommy. Do not worry."

I learned that in 1940 my family was forced to move out of the mansion, and into someone else's house in town. After that, the letters came less frequently. Eventually, instead of letters, I received Red Cross notes from a place called Terezin. They were generic postcards from the Red Cross that said, "Greetings from your family."

Uncle Beda still worked with President Beneš and his government in exile in London. I spent one vacation with him, in 1941, when I was ten years old. He lived in a one-bedroom apartment with his girlfriend. His wife and two children were still alive in Czechoslovakia at the time.

He introduced me to stamp collecting and also to the little stamp shop around the corner from his apartment. For several years I kept stamps, but had little time to work on my collection.

During that visit to London, at night I went to stay at the home of one of Uncle Beda's friends, who had a two-bedroom apartment, but most nights the siren went off, and we all went to the nearest Underground station and slept as best as we could there. The "tube" station acted as an air-raid shelter. After spending most of the night in the shelter, once the "all clear" signal sounded we could go home and back to bed.

During the Second World War I also had contact with my cousin Pauli Cantor. She and her brother had immigrated to London, and she visited me once. I also heard occasionally from Otto Flatter (the uncle who had come to the UK from Vienna with his wife in 1938 when she was the accompanist at some international concert). He would write to me from the Isle of Man, where he had been sent by the British authorities.

For a couple of years, I spent several weeks during the summer at

Uncle Rob's sheep farm near Appin, between Connel and Ben Nevis. Uncle Rob, Mary Corson's father's brother, had been sent to Edinburgh University to study architecture. He made some very good drawings of buildings in Edinburgh, but his real love was for sheep. He left university without graduating and started raising sheep in the countryside. He never married, but he had a housekeeper to take care of the house and cook for his workmen, who lived in a separate building called "the bothy."

I sometimes walked over the hills with the shepherds. I learned to milk cows, and I helped gather the sheep for shearing and dipping. The latter involved immersing the animals in disinfectant to kill parasites. The sheep were gathered into several different pens and were led, group by group, to a pool of water mixed with disinfectant. They swam across this, and my job was to push each head under the liquid before they could come out of the pool at the narrow exit. By the end of the day I had more disinfectant on me than any sheep.

Gathering the sheep was a huge task, but the neighboring farmers helped and made it into a fun-filled project, with a big meal at the end for everyone. Once or twice a week I was sent to the postbox at the end of the country road, about five miles away, to bring the mail home.

On Sundays we walked to the local church. The service was mostly in Gaelic, which I didn't understand. There were no musical instruments, but the precentor would click his tuning fork, find the right note, sing the first line of a psalm, and the congregation sang that line. He would then sing the next line and the congregation would sing on cue, following the leader closely, to the end of the psalm.

Late in 1941, Tom's mother came to visit. She worked as a waitress in London. She made arrangements for him to go to the Czech State Boarding School in Shropshire, England. Before the school year started she suddenly died, but because the arrangements had all been made and it was her wish, Tom was sent to the Czech State School. There he studied with a number of the children who had been rescued by Nicholas Winton.

As I was growing up, I climbed a number of the mountains around Connel and explored some of the countryside. Between Connel and Oban there was a peninsula sticking out into the sea. Here on this peninsula, almost completely hidden among the trees, was the old castle known as Dunstaffnage Castle.

Some of my wanderings in the mountains were in connection with the Boy Scout troop at Dunbeg. I took all my tests and became a "King's Scout." When the base was no longer a naval operation and the military personnel went home, the Scoutmaster left and the scout troop stopped meeting. I tried to run a troop in Connel for a short time, but we didn't attract much interest.

During one outing up in the hills, we had made a fire using just one or two matches, as required by the scouts. I was cutting up some firewood with an axe. One of the scouts moved a big stone to make a seat near the fire, and as he did, a small viper came out of the hole underneath. We could see the "V" marking on its head. With one swipe of the axe in my hand, I chopped off the head of the viper and put it in the fire.

For a short time, I went to the Boy Scout troop in Oban, but as I got more involved in Christian activities I quit scouting.

In the local Church of Scotland magazine there was a children's page with Scripture questions to answer. Miss Corson got me started on these. She taught me how to use Cruden's Concordance, and this led me to take Bible correspondence courses. I found an ad for the "School of Simplified Bible Study." For a teenager this was heavy theology, particularly the section on the epistle to the Romans. I studied the Bible through correspondence courses from the age of 11 until I was 23.

When Tom traveled to the Czech State School in Shropshire, I began attending Oban High School. Oban was a town of about 7,000 people, but was the center of a large agricultural community. Many of the students at the high school came from the surrounding islands and highlands. For a lot of them, English was a second language. Their first language was Gaelic. There were about 1,000 students in the whole school.

I continued to live with Miss Corson, and although I was treated well, I was never part of the family. I was always a guest. I felt very alone until I started going to the monthly Scripture Union meetings and discovered believers among the students in my high school. Once a year, Revd Meikeljohn, the head of Scripture Union, came to speak at the school about the Inter-School Camps. Out of these visits we developed a Scripture Union class after school once a week. I led this meeting for some time. We frequently had outside speakers. We read the Bible passage set by the Scripture Union for that day. I distributed Scripture

Union notes on these daily Bible readings at school and also at the other meetings in which I became involved.

One Sunday Alan Redpath, later the pastor of Moody Church in Chicago, was scheduled to speak in the Oban Baptist Church to tell his story. As a professional rugby player, he had one day missed a pass and failed to score. He was subsequently dropped from the All England rugby team, and his life was completely changed. He went into full-time ministry, and became the pastor of a growing Baptist congregation, which outgrew its church building and started meeting in a theater. He frequently preached at the Keswick Convention in the north of England. I was very keen to hear him speak and so, for this meeting, I was allowed to take the bus, even though it was "breaking the Sabbath."

Alan Redpath gave a very impressive testimony explaining how he had dedicated his life to Jesus Christ on the rugby field. After the meeting, a man called Jimmie Slater invited me to the Monday evening Christian Endeavor (CE) meetings held at the Oban church. Christian Endeavor was an international organization for young people, and our meeting was for anyone aged 14–50 interested in "spiritual growth and discipleship." Certain books of the Bible were studied each year, and everyone took part in the meetings—more than just singing with others—as part of the training. My mentor Jimmie Slater was the leader of this group. One of my tasks was to remind fellow students in high school about the meeting and encourage them to be there.

My heartbeat quickened and my palms grew sweaty as I gathered with others at these meetings. My mouth was dry as I tried to share my thoughts. Every time the study of the book of Amos came up, it was my assignment to teach. Jimmie gave me a commentary on Amos and encouraged me to study it. My efforts at expounding Amos were very warmly received, which encouraged me to do more study and teaching. Soon I was calling him "Uncle Jimmie" and going back into Oban on my bicycle every Sunday and Monday evening.

Uncle Jimmie arranged several trips for our Christian Endeavor members. One was to Glasgow, where some of the older people went shopping and the younger ones enjoyed sightseeing. We had one very memorable picnic on a little island between Oban and the Isle of Mull. We took a motorboat to a quiet beach, and above the beach there was a level field where we played soccer all day, including a game of three-legged soccer.

One Sunday evening a missionary from Congo talked about missionary work. When I got home I went to my room with a little oil lamp. I read in Exodus 13.2, "Consecrate to me every firstborn male. The first offspring . . . belongs to me." God asked for the firstborn of every Jewish family, and I realized that meant me. I had been saved physically from almost certain death in the concentration camps when I took the train to Scotland. I had been saved spiritually when I received Jesus as Savior. I felt God wanted me to be a missionary. At 15 years old I knew my calling, and I was focused on becoming a missionary overseas. Yet even though I was working very hard at my schoolwork, I was barely achieving passing grades. Would this be a problem for my call?

Pushing those worries to the side, I set out to serve God the best I could. I met a young engineer, Jim Crooks, who had been sent to Oban to repair the machines at the ice factory. He came from a Brethren background, was a good preacher, and joined us at the Christian Endeavor meetings. He found several other Brethren families around the countryside and gathered them together, and later a Brethren assembly was formed in Oban.

I also became involved with Faith Mission, a more charismatic group, whose members wore distinctive uniforms and called their workers "pilgrims." The supporters of Faith Mission had a weekly street meeting on Sunday evening right after the church services, followed by an evangelistic meeting in the Mission Hall.

One Friday afternoon when I got out of school, one of the CE leaders, Uncle Archie (Archie MacPhee), was waiting at the gates for me.

"Tommy, on Sunday we would like you to give your testimony at the mission."

Fear gripped me. I wasn't used to talking in front of crowds, and I didn't know how to answer.

"If I'm there, I suppose I can," I finally answered.

Butterflies danced in my stomach on the way home, and my mind raced all evening, attempting to come up with an excuse not to go to the meeting. Failing to find a reason, I lit my little paraffin lamp and went up to my bedroom. Before going to sleep, I turned to the Scripture Union reading for the day, 1 Peter 3.15. The words hit me: "Always be prepared to give an answer to everyone who asks you to give the reason for the hope that you have. But do this with gentleness and respect." It was a verse that didn't leave me, and became central to my life.

That Sunday the room was packed more than normal. The hosts hurried to neighboring houses and apartments to borrow extra chairs. Holding tightly to my Bible, with knees shaking, I told everyone what I knew of my story, about leaving Czechoslovakia as a boy of eight, going from Prague station with a label tied around my neck. It was all I knew.

After my talk I received many invitations to speak at the street meetings, yet during the following week in school, several of my classmates made fun of what I had said and how I said it. At that point, I had never heard of Nicholas Winton. I also never guessed all the places God would call me to share my story in the years to come.

4

After the Second World War
1945–1948

On the day the Second World War ended, I was at Inter-School Camp. There was great rejoicing at the end of the war in Europe. The fighting would cease and soldiers would return. Hitler's reign of terror over our continent had come to an end. I joined the cooks and helpers to prepare a special party, and enjoyed numerous cups of coffee—something that had been rationed during the war.

With the end of the conflict, several of the teachers who had been in the military returned, and sports opportunities increased at the high school. Soccer had been our only sport, but now we started to play basketball, cricket and shinty. Shinty is played in Scotland and Ireland and is something like field hockey.

Among the staff who returned from military service were science teachers. One day when our science teacher was off sick, the teacher from the next class told us to continue with our experiment on our own. Several boys in my class filled a small test-tube with little pellets, sealed the tube, and lit a Bunsen burner under it. We all ducked under the desks, and there was a large explosion. The teacher from the next room, who had come into our lab, was blown over the first countertop and was very shaken by the blast. He was taken to the hospital for care. He had been injured during the war, and the explosion reminded him of the battlefield.

At the end of the Second World War, lists of names were published giving addresses of Czech nationals. A cousin of mine, John, found my address and was very upset to discover that we had both been in the UK all these years and he had done nothing for his young relative. I had vague memories of his visiting us in Těšany during his bicycle trip around Europe in 1937.

John had been in the Czech army in England, but had become a pacifist. He was able to get a discharge from the army and studied statistics at Exeter University. He then applied for immigration papers to join his family—Uncle Arthur, Aunt Emma and Cousin Bob—who had lived in Italy, Spain and Cuba during the war while trying to move to the United States. At the end of the war they were able to get into the USA, and started a chicken farm in Vineland, New Jersey. They invited me to join them, but I was informed that I would have to go to a refugee camp in Europe and apply for immigration as a refugee from there.

Life was far too comfortable in Scotland to think of going to a refugee camp. Cousin John visited me. We took the boat to the head of Loch Etive, cycled from there through Glencoe to Ballachulish, and then boarded a train back to Connel. While cycling through Glencoe, John wanted to stop for a cigarette break. We had been on our bicycles for a couple of hours. As we sat on the grass at the side of the road, he shared some of the family history. He had been raised in Vienna as the son of a prosperous lawyer and educated in a Catholic school. He was not aware of being a Jew until Hitler defined who was to be considered Jewish. For a short time before leaving Czechoslovakia, he had worked in my father's shoe business.

He had a ticket and a date for traveling to the USA. Before he left, he gave me his three-geared bicycle. He joined his family in Vineland, New Jersey, and got a job with the US military in Germany for a couple of years, supervising those who were looking for Nazi war criminals. He returned to the USA and worked for the United Nations, first as a translator and later in the population department.

When John's family received permission to enter the USA, his brother Bob studied in Washington DC and joined the US Navy. On one of his ship's voyages to the UK he visited me in Connel. For most of his later life he worked for the UN in Switzerland, but lived over the border in France.

It was wonderful to meet members of my extended family. Yet even while I was discovering such connections, there was only silence from my home country. Even the Red Cross postcards had stopped in 1942. I didn't want to think about what that meant.

During the Inter-School Camps in 1945, Miss Corson received a letter from Uncle Beda, telling her that all my relatives in Czechoslovakia had died. She forwarded this letter to the camp director, Revd Meikeljohn, so that he could break the news to me.

Revd Meikeljohn sat across from me in his office, and pain was evident on his face.

"I am sorry to tell you, Tommy, that all your family is gone."

I nodded and swallowed down the lump in my throat. We had been waiting so long to hear, and this was to be expected. But just because it was expected news didn't make it easier to receive. Pain filled my chest. I attempted to recall the face of my mother, grandmother and brother, but it hurt too much to do so.

Later, when I was alone, I read the letter from Uncle Beda again. He had just returned from Czechoslovakia, where he had learned that his wife and children had all gone to Auschwitz. Beda broke the dreadful news that everyone from our family who remained behind had died in concentration camps.

Upon his return to Czechoslovakia, Uncle Beda married the widow of another Czech soldier who had been in the UK during the Second World War. Because of her knowledge of English, Aunt Maria was able to become an official translator. She and Uncle Beda had two children, Honza and Michael.

I mourned quietly for my family. Yet, externally, my loss didn't change much. I continued to attend high school, and in 1948, when I was 17 years old, I attended an agricultural summer camp in Selby, Yorkshire.

***

A hot sun warmed my shoulders as I strode through the field lined with hedgerows. The farmer's English accent was new to me, but I guessed I would get used to it soon enough—at least for the summer. I had been sent to work at an agricultural camp in the parish of Selby, near York.

War losses, especially the lack of farmworkers, continued to have an impact on agriculture in the UK, and hundreds of camps such as this dotted the countryside. In our camp, young people had gathered for two months. Laughter carried on the soft winds, yet pain was reflected on our faces. Everyone had known loss. Most, like me, tucked it inside. For as long as most of us could remember, the world had been at war. My story, my loss, was just one of many.

Nissen huts lined the fields, no doubt previously used by soldiers. Nissen huts are barrel-shaped, prefabricated, corrugated iron shelters with cement floors. Just three years earlier, a Royal Air Force base near these farms had been bustling with people, and bombers had filled the air, flying toward Germany. Many planes didn't return. I knew many people had faced loss through those years, but not all had responded to Christ as I had.

For two months we would wake before dawn and eat quickly, then line up and wait for the trucks to arrive. These large trucks carried us straight into the fields. Supervisors were waiting there, and they directed our day's work. At evening, the trucks returned and carried us back. And for most of the workers, this was when the fun began.

The summer night's air was hot and sticky as I sat beside my bed and read my Bible. Few gave me even a cursory glance as they headed out to the local pubs.

I saw for the first time how young people lived in this world. They drank too much, complained of headaches the next day, and often boasted of their sexual exploits. Others were remorseful for what they had done, and I noticed deep regret in their eyes. Did they wonder, as I did, how life would be different if there hadn't been a war? Sometimes my thoughts took me back to Těšany.

Every summer, as a child, I had spent a lot of time in the fields with my father's men as they supervised the workers. Karel drove a tractor for harvesting and always had a padded seat on the right wheel cover for me. We gathered cherries as a family, along with our house servants. Often when we were in the fields I would be dropped off with Maria, Karel's daughter, at a row of housing provided for the seasonal workers. The Slovak and Ruthenian women would give us brown bread spread with goose or pork fat. Many years later Maria reminded me that whenever Mother made me a slice of bread and butter, she would give Maria a slice with pork fat, and we used to exchange them.

When the main harvest was brought in, the seasonal workers, accompanied by a brass band, marched from the courtyard to the front entrance of our house carrying a wreath of wheat and other gifts for our family, before they went home.

The weather in 1939—right before my departure—was unusual. Heavy rains destroyed many of the wheat fields. I vividly remember going to a field with my stepfather while the workers were harvesting root crops, when suddenly a violent hailstorm pounded us. Julius drove the car under the shelter of a wall-less barn. The women in the fields emptied their baskets, put them over their heads, and ran for cover. A couple of them fell to the ground, and I was later told they had died from injuries caused by the huge hailstones.

In 1939 we had a big crop of peas to harvest, and workers' kids were invited to help gather the peas from the field. This was my first paid employment, even though it wasn't much.

In Těšany we also had a huge garden, with a sandbox where Tony and I played with neighborhood kids. There were wide paths between the rows of vegetables and flowerbeds. The sandbox was near a greenhouse where plants thrived. Further back there was a beehive. We were warned not to go near it.

Yet now I was no longer a child, and instead of looking back, my mind was set on the call God had given me to be a missionary. I decided to focus on sharing the gospel wherever God placed me.

When Sunday arrived, most people at the agricultural camp slept in, but I climbed on my bicycle, which I had been allowed to bring. My heart was longing to gather with other Christians and to hear God's word taught. I didn't know where I was headed as I rode, and joy filled me when I came upon a Salvation Army "Open Air" street meeting in progress.

I joined the circle and was invited to share my testimony. The members gave a big welcome to the little Jewish boy who had left Prague with the label around his neck. I attended their meetings regularly and enjoyed fellowship with the Salvation Army throughout that summer.

Yet even as I worked at the agricultural summer camp, I had no idea my cousin Lisl had come to Scotland. At great expense, she had traveled by ship to take me to live with her and her family back in Australia. Yet they had no way to find me.

"I was so upset when I couldn't contact you, Tommy," she told me years later. "It had been a very expensive trip. Our whole family was making a very big sacrifice to bring you home with us." She smiled at me. "But that's what family is about."

How would my life have changed if Lisl had made contact? Everything would have been different. I know that.

5

Preparing to be a missionary
1948–1953

The man stood erect before us with a broad smile and squared shoulders. A hint of the soldier he had been during the war was evident. Major Ian Thomas had been a very active witness for the Lord during his military career, including a stint in Germany. He established a Bible school at Capernwray in the north of England, and a friendship group for his students called the Capernwray Fellowship. Even though he was used to addressing large crowds, he had come to speak at our small gathering in Oban.

I looked around the classroom where we met for our Christian Endeavor meetings, and my heart beat a bit faster. The room was filled— far more than usual—and I marveled at how effortlessly Major Thomas told his story of wanting to serve God, and working so hard to do so as a high school and college student, only to have God speak to his heart.

"'You see, for seven years, with utmost sincerity, you have been trying to live for me, on my behalf.' I felt God speak this to my heart," said Major Thomas. "But it was a life that God had been waiting for seven years to live through me."

He went on, sharing how, instead of trying to act in a godly manner, each of us young people simply needed to open our lives to God, and to let God be God in us and through us. The room was quiet, and it seemed everyone was taking in the words. I only hoped that I could share the gospel in such a way someday—that my words would make a difference, like those of Major Thomas and other preachers who had been drawn to the area since the end of the war.

My connection with these great men of God started because every summer Alan Redpath—the evangelist who had given his life to the Lord on a rugby field—came to Oban for a vacation, and Uncle Jimmie used to take him out fishing in Oban Bay. Alan liked the town, so he organized a local conference. He invited several good preachers to speak: Duncan Campbell, Major Ian Thomas and his brother, Guy King, and H. W. Cragg.

The conference had been held for three years in a row, and every evening after the meeting the Oban Christian Endeavor team had to clear people from the sidewalk that extended from the back of the church to the front door. Alan Redpath would pronounce the benediction, come out of the back door, run down the sidewalk, and be ready to shake hands with people leaving the meeting. Then there was an after-meeting in the small back hall behind the church. Our CE group gave out refreshments. This kind of meeting was called a "squash" because it involved many people in a very small area. After the refreshments there was singing and another special speaker.

This year, Major Ian Thomas and his brother had both given talks, and they told jokes about each other. I had asked Alan Redpath if he could speak at my Scripture Union class during the week of the conference, but instead he sent Major Thomas. Now the students in the room were listening intently, and at the end of the major's talk, one of my classmates accepted the Lord.

Eagerness filled me, and I longed to be as knowledgeable about the Bible as these men of God. Now in my last year at high school, I wrote to the Bible Training Institute (BTI) in Glasgow about enrolling. Disappointment set in when the principal of the Institute advised me to get work experience first. But, after considering numerous options, I decided to become a nurse. I heard of a training school at Hairmyres, near Hamilton in Lanarkshire, Scotland, and sent in my application.

At Easter 1948 there was a Christian Endeavor convention in Hamilton, and Uncle Jimmie invited me to go with him. I went to Hairmyres Hospital to be interviewed by the Senior Nursing Director the day before the convention. My nervousness over how the interview went was soon replaced by great joy over the CE meeting, followed by great worry over my accommodation for the week.

After the first evening meeting, everyone from out of town had to find a family to give us hospitality over the weekend. As I scanned the room, hoping someone would claim me, a young lady, Rita Liddle, approached.

"Are you Tom Graumann?"

"Yes."

She held out a very cold hand to shake. It felt like a dead fish. "You'll be staying with my family," she answered curtly.

I swallowed a lump in my throat. Would her family give me the same chilly welcome?

Along with other young people, we walked a long way to Upper Blantyre. Relief flooded me when we arrived at our destination, and Rita's parents threw open the door with warm smiles. Rita's father Willy Liddle was badly crippled with arthritis, but he was able to work as night watchman at the local coal mine. As we got to know each other over the coming days, I learned he was a deacon in the Baptist church who frequently preached and taught its youth group. Also, the family lived only a mile from Blantyre, the birthplace of the famous Scottish missionary to central Africa, David Livingstone.

After that, I visited Blantyre many times. When David Livingstone was growing up, his family was involved in weaving and had a two-roomed apartment in a building owned by the weaving company. As he took care of the mechanized looms, David read many books. He later studied medicine at Glasgow University and went to central Africa, where he was a great explorer, anti-slavery activist and preacher. Sadly, his mission board, the London Missionary Society, fired him because he had no "converts." But he went back to Africa as a representative of the Queen and continued preaching the gospel to the tribes he came across in his explorations.

Two things David Livingstone wrote impressed me very much as I prepared to be a missionary: "God had only one Son and he made that Son a missionary" and "I'll go anywhere as long as it is forward."

After the Christian Endeavor convention, Uncle Jimmie gave a general report to church members. He also asked me to give a report of the messages, about which I had taken notes. One message I especially liked was based on the command of Jesus, "Launch out into the deep." My soul confirmed the words of the message. I needed to go into service for God and not be held back by failure.

As missionary William Carey stated: "Attempt great things for God. Expect great things from God."

I took this as confirmation that I should go to Hairmyres Hospital, train as a nurse, and prepare to become a missionary. Nursing was the first step of my training. The wholehearted dedication of Major Thomas, William Carey and David Livingstone spurred me on.

***

Hairmyres Hospital had previously been a military hospital, and I was in one of the first groups of civilian students accepted. It had been built out in the countryside for soldiers suffering from tuberculosis. The female nurses' home and administration buildings were substantial. There were three large buildings, but most of the remaining units were Nissen huts, with coke-burning stoves down the middle of the one-roomed wards— pretty rough conditions.

We started with a three-month orientation course, which was full-time study. After that, we took three-month rotations in different units to provide us with wide experience. My rotation repeatedly took me to the men's urology and chest surgery departments. The open-heart surgeries bothered me the most. Often I read in the doctor's charts, "The surgery was successful. However, the patient died."

On my first day of nurses' training at the hospital, I accompanied other student nurses, saw what they were doing, and learned basic nursing skills such as shaving patients, giving bed baths, making beds, setting trays up for various procedures, and equipping a trolley for distributing medicine.

From day one I was taught to give intramuscular injections, and I helped with changing dressings. Because there were 27–30 patients in one room, with no treatment rooms, we took a set of screens to a patient's bedside, screened off the patient, and explained what we were going to do. While one nurse scrubbed his or her hands for the procedure, another took off the old dressing.

Half of the nurses in my class were men. The housing for men and women was kept well separated. In the men's quarters, there were two beds in each room. At the end of the hall, there were bathrooms, toilets and a little kitchen. My roommate was Matt Davidson. He had been a fitter-turner in an engineering factory but, because of the low wages, had turned to nursing. He found me very naive and was a big help to me as

I entered the working world. Matt was a believer, attended a charismatic church, and had a Thompson Chain Reference Bible which we often shared as we discussed our different beliefs.

Even though Rita's cool welcome had worried me at first, I found myself a frequent visitor to her family's home. In addition, Jim Crooks and his wife Nellie were like second parents to me. I felt comfortable in their home, and listened to. Their approval and prayers spurred me on. Nellie Crooks' father, John Donaldson, whom I called "Uncle John," was the choir leader of their church. Not long after I moved to Lanarkshire, I had started attending their assembly, and also Faith Mission where Mr Naismith Sr gave a series of lectures on "Church Doctrine and Practice." One evening he spoke about baptism, and something stirred within me. I had never seen adult baptism but I had studied the teaching. Knowing it was a practice I wanted to follow, Uncle John baptized me after the message.

Soon I joined the choir so I could participate in the Saturday evening "tea meetings" where members of the choir sang and spoke. Tea meetings were usually preceded by street meetings, inviting people to attend. The program included choir songs, testimonies and a short evangelistic message. During the meeting, everyone was always served a cup of tea and something to eat.

Sunday evening began with a prayer. Then everyone marched out to the crossroads or a housing development, where people were often standing around. There would be some singing and a short message, and someone would invite the listeners to join us for an evangelistic meeting at the Gospel Hall. Then we set off back to the chapel with Uncle John leading the singing as we marched. All over the county of Lanarkshire there were about 60 Open Brethren assemblies with a similar program. Jim Crooks was invited to preach in many of these assemblies, and I went along.

Several years before I moved to Lanarkshire, four young men—Jim Crooks, Willy Wilding, Bill Hamilton and Willy Freel—had met in front of the Motherwell post office. Feeling called to reach the youth of their community, they decided to hold a meeting the next Sunday evening in that very location, and they invited their friends to join them.

By the time I joined, there were 100–200 young people meeting every Sunday evening. The speakers had a simple public address system, and their message could be heard by those outside waiting for a bus. Often some of us would gather with little preparation, take a bus to a nearby village, speak to people standing around the crossroads, and distribute gospel tracts.

We had a few hecklers, but in our group there were several six-foot-tall guys who would surround the troublemakers, at which point they fell quiet. The hecklers soon started to listen, and one of their leaders later ended up in full-time Christian work.

Many came to believe in Christ, including one young illiterate guy who traveled to all the assemblies, sharing his testimony. A changed person, he attended Bible college, partly to learn to read and write. The spiritual revival of the street preaching was evident, and in my nursing I also witnessed something miraculous.

During my training, new drugs were developed for the treatment of tuberculosis. Some of the patients, who had been unable to speak for as much as 25 years, were able to speak again. Joy filled their faces as they uttered words they had held inside and hadn't been able to give voice to. Tears ran down the faces of family members to hear the voices of their loved ones that had been silenced for so long.

How amazing it was for me to witness the cure for tuberculosis, which had plagued Scotland for many years. But this was not the only disease that crippled our country: another was polio. A vaccine was developed, and the epidemic was stopped, but we still had to treat many who had paralysis as a result of having had this condition.

***

Summer vacation gave me a break from my studies, but not from work. Growing up, I had always enjoyed the Inter-School Camps, and now it seemed all my hands-on training would be put to good use, as Uncle Jimmie and I joined forces to help a man named Sandy Barbour.

Sandy came from Oban, and he was a very gifted musician. During the Second World War he had served in the British Navy and played professional soccer. In preparation for church planting in France, he conducted children's campaigns and evangelized around the European Christian Mission headquarters at Heightside, in northern England. Sandy was soon asked to run a camp for children saved during his evangelistic meetings, and he recruited Uncle Jimmie to help. Since neither Sandy nor Uncle Jimmie knew how to pitch bell-tents, I joined them.

I went to Heightside with Uncle Jimmie, and we stayed in the dormitory for male missionaries. I was really impressed the next morning when we were served a full English breakfast, including bacon, eggs and toast! After breakfast we helped wash up the dishes, then joined the other missionaries in the prayer room. The men prayed for the children's camp, and then they prayed for funds to come in for ECM so that the missionaries could eat the next day. They prayed with faith, and later that day the mail brought in the needed funds.

After breakfast we went to the next town, and found the tents and equipment Sandy had ordered for camp being loaded onto a huge truck. Several of us sat on the top of the vehicle, and we traveled across northern England to the coastal village of Skipsea to set up the camp.

Soon a chartered bus arrived with 80 campers. Two ladies, who had fed Sandy very well during a previous series of meetings, had volunteered to cook. They had a small pump-up camp stove and a quart pan of fat. They worked for two hours frying "chips" (French fries), but we soon discovered they only had enough food for half of the campers before the evening meeting. The others had to wait for their chips until after the meeting that night.

The next morning Jimmie, Sandy and I were in the prayer tent, praying about the problem of feeding all these campers, when these two ladies approached.

"I'm sorry, but this is more than we can do," one woman explained. "We're not going to be able to stay and cook after all."

With that apology, she and her companion said their goodbyes, and we were left on our own with this unexpected problem.

The other men were silent, but I jumped to my feet.

"Can you have the campers gather firewood?" I asked, and without hesitation I hurried to the cookhouse. I cooked the food on hand, and Uncle Jimmie went to town and bought more supplies. That became our routine. Uncle Jimmie would shop. He bought vegetables, potatoes, eggs and milk from local farmers. The food was very simple, and bread was cheap. He also preached each evening at the meetings, and I set to work cooking for all the campers and staff.

Thankfully, the farmer who owned this property was a Christian, eager to use his fields for the Lord's service. Inside the little cookhouse was a small stove, the size you would find in an apartment, which ran on propane. There was also a sink with cold water, but the drain just went into the ground beside the cookhouse. There was a table and bench, and little more. All of this was useful, but it was still inadequate for the numbers we had, and so we also needed to cook over a fire outside.

Uncle Jimmie and I put up a tarpaulin for shelter from the wind and a partial roof over the open fire. I cooked in large pots the best I could, but it was hard to make pancakes while the rain poured down.

After the first camp, Stuart Harris, Director of ECM, invited Uncle Jimmie to join ECM as a children's evangelist. Uncle Jimmie wasn't sure about leaving his business in the hands of his brothers and going out "in faith" after being a successful businessman for several years.

I was at home in Connel that Christmas, and I went with Uncle Jimmie to the New Year's Day Faith Mission Conference at Fort William. The message came from Luke 5, and challenged us to "Launch out into the deep." The same message that had impressed me affected Uncle Jimmie too. He took this as his call to work with ECM. So he left his business to his brothers, packed up his things, and moved to Heightside. He did anything that needed doing at the headquarters, and conducted children's missions in churches all over Scotland and the north of England.

I helped Uncle Jimmie at his camps for several years. There were a number of fine young people trained to be tent leaders during these gatherings. A teacher from a town nearby brought several children from her school. One girl, Pat, came from a godless background. On the second night of camp she accepted the Lord. Shortly afterwards she read a leaflet I had in my possession, written by Oswald Smith of Toronto. It said, "No one has a right to hear the gospel twice, before everyone has heard it once."

Pat said, "That can't be right. I didn't accept Jesus till the second time I heard the gospel."

She was a completely changed girl and had grown a lot spiritually by the end of camp. When she got home her parents were furious. They took her Bible away, forbade her to have anything to do with the Christians at her school, and started to sue Uncle Jimmie for "brainwashing" their daughter. Uncle Jimmie was able to talk to her parents and the legal suit was stopped, but Pat wasn't allowed to own a Bible, even though there were Bible lessons provided at her school.

One of the highlights of camp was the bonfire on the last night, when everyone had an opportunity to share what camp meant to them and to tell about their spiritual experience. We always ended by singing together:

I have decided to follow Jesus,
No turning back, no turning back.

The world behind me, the cross before me:
No turning back, no turning back.
(Attributed to Sadhu Sundar Singh, 1889–1929)

If there was nothing else going on Saturday evening, I would catch the bus into Glasgow and attend the meeting called "Saturday Evening at 7," which was held at the Tent Hall. This was a ministry started after the Moody and Sankey meetings in Glasgow in 1874. The Tent Hall particularly ministered to the poor, and offered free meals and other assistance. On Saturday evenings hundreds of young people from churches all around Glasgow would bring their friends to hear the gospel. Special speakers came for these meetings. One evening, John Moore, the superintendent, brought a little pump organ to the front of the platform and sat down to play. He sang a new song he had just written, a song about casting our cares on Jesus today. The verses spoke of having sorrows and cares, worries and fears. The message resonated deeply with the crowd.

The umbrella organization for the ministries coming out of the Moody campaign was the Glasgow Evangelistic Association. This organization invited Billy Graham for a six-week crusade in 1954. (More on this below.)

While at Hairmyres Hospital, I took every opportunity to share my testimony, including my call to be a missionary. At the end of my time there, I talked to four of the seven elders of Faith Mission. Each one of them told me that when my request for commendation to be a missionary came up, he would support me. However, when the elders got together to discuss my desire to go to the field, they decided against it. On behalf of the elders, John Donaldson wrote, "This assembly has never sent out a missionary in the fifty years of its existence and we're not going to start now."

Sadness filled me. I knew the response had little to do with the call to send out missionaries. Instead, it was more about one strong-willed person within the group of elders, persuading everyone else to reject me.

The door had slammed shut, and I didn't understand why. Wasn't this God's call? It had been my focus since I was a young boy.

Still, I felt very confident with my nursing knowledge and skills, and I tried to stay positive about my future. At the end of three years at Hairmyres I took my board exams. Immediately, I started a course in orthopedic nursing for graduate nurses at Killearn Hospital in Stirlingshire, even though I still didn't have my license. I was one of two graduate nurses, and we competed for all the exams. When I graduated, the instructor asked me what book I would like as a prize for orthopedic nursing, so I asked for *Systematic Theology* by A. H. Strong.

After this, I signed up as a registered nurse at an orthopedic hospital. I worked as a registered nurse for about six months before my official nursing license papers came.

Even as I continued with nursing, at the next assembly I again asked the church elders to send me out to the mission field. For the second time, they said no. Undaunted, I applied once more to the Bible Training Institute in Glasgow. I felt called to go, regardless of the church's response. This time I was accepted! I paid for my studies, also qualifying for a grant (called a bursary) from the District Board of Education that did not have to be repaid.

While at Bible school, I attended missionary meetings relating to every part of the world, and prayer meetings with every mission organization in Glasgow, including those for Worldwide Evangelism Crusade where I prayed regularly with Brother Andrew, who would later become famous as "God's smuggler." Even as I had trained to bring health and healing to bodies, my greatest desire continued to be to bring many souls to Christ.

6

Glasgow and Liverpool
1954

Eagerness stirred within me. In a matter of days the truth of God's love would be shared on a scale I had never experienced before. The American evangelist Billy Graham had come to Glasgow for a six-week crusade, and I was to be a part of it.

For the last year I had been attending the Bible Training Institute in the city. The Institute ran a two-year course with an emphasis on foreign missions. Andrew MacBeath, a missionary returned from Africa, had just been chosen as the principal. He required every student to teach a Sunday school class. No matter what part of the world we went to, there would be lots of children.

Many churches in the Glasgow area invited teams of international students to speak at meetings. We also conducted Saturday street meetings at an open-air market called Barrowland.

One of my fellow students, Rochunga Pudaite, from India, was invited to many meetings. In his messages, there was very little explanation of the gospel. Any one of us could have given a fuller exposition, but wherever he went people received the Lord.

Rochunga came from the mountains of Assam, India, where the Hmar people live. He was well educated in his homeland, with degrees in philosophy. He had also studied English for 19 years. As we studied the Bible, he discovered that many English words did not mean what he thought they meant, and he needed to change a lot of things in the Hmar translation of the New Testament.

While in Glasgow, Rochunga frequently visited the American consulate to request a visa for the USA, where the Bible Society wanted him to study. For political reasons, the USA was not giving visas to people from

India. Finally, he made a last appointment. The consul immediately told him, "You cannot get a visa for the USA."

Rochunga responded, "I have made a half-hour appointment. Let's talk about some of my American friends in India."

He had many influential friends in high office in India and knew many of the US consuls. They talked about these mutual friends—and he left the consulate with a visa for the USA.

Another very gifted student was Wolfgang Schroeder. The youngest member of the East German Communist Parliament, he had been sent to monitor meetings conducted by Major Ian Thomas. During the major's time in the military he had conducted seminars for soldiers where he explained the gospel, and many accepted the Lord.

After the war, Major Thomas set up a Bible school in the north of England. He attracted young soldiers and young Germans to his seminars, and the East German Parliament was interested in getting a report about what he was doing—investigating him prior to shutting him out of their own country. However, Wolfgang ran away from his duties, having come to Christ, and obtained asylum in the UK. Later he requested permission to attend youth meetings in England, where he accepted Jesus as Lord and Savior. After graduating, he went to Switzerland to plant a German-speaking church.

Now I gathered with these and other friends to prepare for Billy Graham's arrival. I knew what an impact this event could make because 12 of my fellow students were new believers. All 12 of them had trusted in Jesus as Savior at the Billy Graham meetings at Wimbledon in 1952.

Every student at BTI attended counseling classes, and most of us became counselors or ushers, or both, at the upcoming crusade. The night before Billy Graham arrived, we had an all-night prayer meeting, which was open to the public. In the morning, we all went to the railway station to welcome Billy Graham.

Billy appeared, wearing a dark suit, and looked at us with an expression of hope.

"The whole world is praying for Glasgow," he said. "There will be unusual opportunities to witness." Billy smiled. "I don't expect to save Glasgow, but even if we get dirty again, taking a bath is a good thing."

Shortly after Billy Graham arrived, he called for a special meeting for all the workers. When all the choir members, counselors, advisors, prayer-group members and ushers had assembled, we completely filled Kelvin Hall, the exhibition center in Glasgow's West End where the crusade would be held.

Billy stood, and his eyes scanned the room as he leaned over the podium.

"I am concerned about the advertising all over this city," his low voice rumbled. "'Hear Billy Graham!' May Billy Graham not receive the glory, but God! As we read in Isaiah forty-two, 'I am the Lord. That is my name and I will not give my glory to another.'"

My chest filled with warmth as I listened to him preach, and then together we sang the motto selected for these meetings: "Let Glasgow flourish by the preaching of the word and the praising of his name." This motto hung on the outside of the stadium. On all the city equipment, such as the city buses, a shorter version was printed: "Let Glasgow flourish."

Several of us went daily to the Billy Graham headquarters and stuffed envelopes with literature to send to people who had contributed or written to the office. Excitement built as the first day of the crusade neared.

The seating at Kelvin Hall was limited, so churches and individuals had to request tickets. I stood in line for hours to get tickets for friends. Churches arranged buses to bring groups to the meetings. My friend, Jim Crooks, sang in the choir.

On the opening night of the first crusade meeting, I acted as an usher and sat in a seat assigned for me. Electricity filled the air as Billy Graham's words blared over the speakers:

Our political and military leaders have said, repeatedly, they do not know the answer to the present world dilemma. Its uncertainty is beginning to penetrate to the man on the street. The average man must turn somewhere. He must have some faith and hope to hold on to. Thousands are turning to God and are finding peace, security, happiness and joy in this age of uncertainty and confusion.

After the sermon, a mass choir sang a version of the Lord's Prayer as Billy Graham announced, "I'm going to ask people to come forward . . ."

Those of us who were counselors bowed our heads and popped a mint into our mouths, as we had been instructed. Hundreds of people from all over the auditorium surged forward. I went to the front, looked for a guy without a counselor's badge, and stood beside him. I was shaking with the excitement of this opportunity. After a few words and a prayer, we walked into the counseling room, and I led a man to Christ.

During the crusade, I had the privilege of leading several people to the Lord. Almost all of these men had started attending church in the year before the crusade and had been searching for God for some time.

The churches of England and Scotland were no longer as full as they had been. There were still countless numbers of people who needed the gospel, and my burden to share God's truth grew.

At the Bible Training Institute, missionary prayer meetings were held early every morning for different parts of the world. I attended all of these and studied a lot about missionary work in Europe. Since I had several friends in the European Christian Mission, and had stayed at their headquarters several times, everyone assumed I was going to Europe with that organization. Yet, as I looked at Czechoslovakia under Communist control, I decided I would never return there. How could I ever go back within those borders while the country was under such oppression?

The mission group that gave the most information for prayer and put the least pressure on students to join it was the Overseas Missionary Fellowship (OMF). I enjoyed the prayer group run by its members and felt attracted to the Philippines. They specifically prayed for God to bring forward single, healthy men who could hike deep into the mountains and rainforests. Warmth filled my chest. I could do that.

At the Far East prayer meeting, we prayed for former students now missionaries in the Philippines. The Sutherlands had pioneered a ministry on the island of Palawan, and during the Second World War they hid in the forested interior. Their children kept praying for a submarine to rescue them from the Japanese, who had invaded the Philippines. The Lord answered that prayer, and a submarine came to their island and took them to Australia. After the war was over, the family was able to return, and continued to minister and plant churches among the Palawano people of the Philippines.

My heart stirred again, but there was a problem. I wasn't a linguist. We had a week of practical experience learning a foreign language from a native speaker known as an "informant." The individual I was assigned to was my classmate Rochunga Pudaite. He had done some translation into the Hmar language of Assam, India, but my own language skills that week were a dismal failure. How would I ever be called overseas when I struggled so much?

Still, I continued to take steps of faith, trusting that if God had given me the desire, he would provide the way.

After the midterm exam, we had a long weekend off. During this weekend I had scheduled a visit to Sefton General Hospital, in Liverpool, to enroll in the Tropical Nursing course. I prayed about it and felt sure that it was God's will, but I didn't have the money to get there.

Very eagerly on the Saturday morning, I opened the only letter that had arrived for me in the mail, thinking that perhaps the envelope would contain a gift of money. In it was a tract entitled, "Others May, You Cannot." Among the things it said was this: "Others may be allowed to succeed in making money . . . but it is likely that God will keep you poor."

I might be poor, but I placed my trust in a God who owned everything. Still without the money I needed, I packed and went to the bathroom to get cleaned up. When I returned to my bed, I found the exact fare, by train, to Liverpool lying on my suitcase. Sending up a prayer of thanksgiving, I took the overnight train to Liverpool and arrived in time for my interview in the morning.

Afterwards, I walked along the river and heard a man preaching the gospel, and I joined him. He and I preached a number of times. When he had said all he wanted to say, he would start singing. His singing wasn't very good, but it was an effective way to end the meeting. He then started to preach again and more people gathered. After several hours, he invited me to his home for dinner and to stay the night.

Soon, I found myself studying tropical nursing at Sefton General Hospital, a part of Liverpool University. We had a number of people being treated for a variety of diseases, including malaria. As a research exercise, one of the doctors brought a box with a number of tropical mosquitoes, placed it on a patient, and after a few bites took the box away. We then treated the man for malaria, including sponging him down when he developed a high fever. The nurses had to get 30 blood slides from each patient when the person developed a fever—one for each of the student doctors!

Not only did this procedure help us understand how to manage tropical diseases, but it was also at the time considered an experimental treatment. The medical staff believed this was a valid approach for several different diseases. They encouraged patients to get a fever, and then treated the fever, in order to "cure" other ailments, such as kidney disease.

There were a number of Pakistani sailors who checked into the hospital after a rough voyage and wanted a rest from sailing. It was easy to find a number of different parasites afflicting these men, for which they were soon treated.

During my time in Liverpool, I was able to speak at a number of meetings of the Nurses Christian Fellowship in different hospitals around the city. Together with several other Christians taking the Tropical Nursing course, I started a Nurses Christian Fellowship at Sefton General Hospital, but before long I was moving on again.

I applied to the Overseas Missionary Fellowship, and was accepted by the Glasgow office and went to London for a three-month orientation program. After that, I would be sent overseas, where I would learn about the country where I would serve and start language school. Finally, my turn had come to go into the world.

My fellow students and I lived at the old mission home at Newington Green, north London. We studied the history of the China Inland Mission and the history and geography of all the "new fields" in which the OMF was starting work. We had lectures from missionaries and also London preachers.

We were all assigned to local churches for ministry opportunities. I taught a midweek children's class at a nearby Plymouth Brethren assembly. One of the elders told me before I started, "Don't say anything if the children are rowdy. When the last missionaries did that, some boys got angry and threw stones and broke some windows."

While at Newington Green we made several "field trips" to a retirement home for former OMF and China Inland Mission missionaries, called

Cornford House, near Tunbridge Wells in Kent. Some of these veteran missionaries had been involved in the anti-missionary Boxer riots at the turn of the twentieth century.

Every morning we prayed for China and the new OMF fields. It was great to hear the retired missionaries pray. They prayed for specific provinces of China on each day of the week, and many of them prayed by name for Chinese Christian leaders in these provinces. The person leading the prayer-time read the names of the missionaries and where they were located. We prayed specifically for each person and for his or her ministry.

After the orientation program, we had a number of months to prepare ourselves, raise our prayer-support team, and pack our boxes for our trip to Singapore, where our training would continue. I joined Uncle Jimmie for a while in Aberdeen and several other towns along the east coast of Scotland.

I remember kneeling down to pray one time with Uncle Jimmie. We were both penniless. He had some meetings in Aberdeen churches scheduled, but we had nothing to eat. While we were praying, we heard some noise outside Uncle Jimmie's "caravan," a small trailer in which we were living. There on the step, we found a big bag of sausages and other kinds of meat, a gift from a dedicated butcher.

I went home to Connel to pack the wooden boxes that I had been issued at OMF with most of the things on their outfit list. I planned to have pants (trousers) made in Singapore when I got there. The Oban Christian Endeavor group arranged a number of meetings for me in prayer groups in little villages around Oban. Many times, I showed a film about the start of the missionary work on the island of Mindoro.

My friend Jim Crooks wanted to have a farewell meeting for me, so while he and some other friends talked about arrangements for this meeting, I led one of Jim's scheduled children's meetings. That night there were six children who wanted to make decisions for Christ. I talked to them and prayed with each of them individually. I returned to Jim Crooks' house walking on air.

When we arrived at the YMCA hall in Motherwell, which Jim had booked for the farewell meeting, we found the chairs all neatly stacked at the side. The manager explained that, since this was to be a farewell, he expected it would be a dance, so the staff had cleared the floor. We got the seating lined up again and soon the room was well filled. Jim Crooks had found several people who had a special connection with me, and they all said nice things about me!

That night, after the meeting, I was returning to London on an overnight train. Most of the people at my farewell meeting came to the train station to see me off and sang the hymn, "Great Is Thy Faithfulness."

As the train was pulling out of the station, one of my male nurse friends, Joe Wilson, ran along the platform next to the train and said, "Remember God's faithfulness. We may forget you, but he won't."

Before leaving for Singapore, all those from the UK and USA who were going together to Singapore stayed for a few days at the OMF home in Newington Green, and we all participated in meetings around London. Jim and Nellie Crooks, and Jim Anderson, came to London to be with me as I was leaving. Jim Anderson was a fellow disciple of Jim Crooks. They accompanied us to Southampton and saw us board the ship that would take us to Singapore. I was dressed in my kilt as I left. Scotland had prepared me for the mission to come.

7

Central Language School
1955

The book lay open on my lap, but the words seemed to swim on the page. My head pounded, but I forced myself to continue. My mouth moved, attempting to mimic the sounds I had learned earlier that way, but it was useless. How could I ever remember these strange words? Eager to learn, I poured myself into my studies, but it did little good. With a frustrated sigh I closed the book and placed it on the desk.

I stood and looked out of the window, reminding myself I was in Singapore, and this was my one chance to prepare as an overseas missionary. A garden city, where East meets West—if all went well this place would be my home for only a few months. After a series of interviews with OMF directors, to determine which country we were going to be assigned to and which language we were to study, I had my mind set on the Philippines and was required to study Tagalog.

While at the Central Language School, we were all assigned to work with a church in Singapore. I was invited to teach an English Sunday school in a Chinese church. The children attending this Sunday school went to English school and didn't know how to read Chinese.

I also started a teacher training class. This was a good learning experience, and I was invited to the homes of several of these students. Some of them lived in big high-rise apartments, so different from the seaside villages of Scotland. The city was well designed and beautiful. Yet even in this modern city there were still many poor people, and my heart ached for their needs.

The food in Singapore was a big change, and I ate Chinese food for the first time. It was very tasty! There were Chinese cooks at the language school, and I even learned to eat it standing on the street with a banana leaf as a plate.

One day, I invited a couple of the young women from the teacher training class to the language school for dinner. They were as perplexed about our food as I had been about theirs.

"You do things backwards," they commented. "The meat you serve in a big slab, and the fruit you cut up into little pieces. We cut meat into bite-sized pieces, and we eat fruit the way it grows, whole."

Another time, one of our Filipino teachers invited us to dinner for a traditional Filipino meal. We had rice with a sweet and sour sauce and vegetables. She had stocked her refrigerator with beer, expecting us to drink a lot of it, and had difficulty finding us other cold drinks.

It was monsoon season. The weather was nice, clear and bright every morning, with the temperature rising. Then around one or two in the afternoon there would be a heavy downpour of rain, followed by a pleasant evening. Most of us played volleyball and then studied in the evening.

In our Tagalog class we had one engaged couple, Phil and Margaret. Many members of our Central Language School group were engaged, but OMF did not allow these engaged couples to get married until they had completed the basic language course.

I didn't consider marriage. When I first felt the call to be a missionary, I had heard a speaker in Glasgow preach from 1 Corinthians 9. The apostle Paul didn't exercise his right to marriage, and this speaker emphasized that the OMF was looking for single men able to climb mountains to reach people in faraway places. That's what my sights were set on.

Most people around me suffered from homesickness, but there was no real home for me to look back to. I did receive letters from Miss Corson and Uncle Jimmie, and there were many who promised to pray for me, and I tried to keep in touch.

Once a week, we all went to a weekly prayer meeting at the OMF headquarters on Cluny Road. We met all the missionaries working in the city of Singapore. At one of these meetings we heard that the New Tribes Mission had handed over to OMF the responsibility of evangelizing the south of the island of Mindoro. For several years they had held a boot camp there for the training of missionaries to work with new tribes. They now wanted to move their boot camp to another island. We were told that we had five to ten years to evangelize the island, and after that it would fall to the Communists. My friend Nick Wehren felt particularly called to that ministry, and I wondered if I would soon find myself there too.

***

After five months at language school, the five-member Tagalog language-group received exit papers to leave Singapore, and visas to enter the Philippines. A missionary named Frances Williamson and her sister Mabel were in Singapore working on a book. During language school she had come and shared simple stories about missionary life in the Philippines as one of our conversation classes in Tagalog. She accompanied us to the country.

We were on a French ship, which stopped for three days at Saigon. We had an interesting visit there and saw a very different culture. We also met some of the Vietnamese Christians.

When we arrived in Manila, Sam Jeffrey, the business manager, was at the pier to welcome us and take us to the Manila mission home. His wife Signe was the mission home hostess. They had both served for many years in China and had numerous stories about missionary work there. Sam took us to the various government offices and got us through customs and immigration proceedings. He also took us to a number of places around Manila to introduce us to the capital.

We visited the Far East Broadcasting Company studio, DZAS, at Karuhatan, where OMF missionaries work, broadcasting news and Bible-teaching programs throughout the Philippines and into China and other Far East countries. One program, *Radio Bible School*, offered Emmaus Bible correspondence courses, and thousands of Filipinos were enrolled on these courses.

On our first Sunday morning in the Philippines, we went to Grace Bible Church where we met missionaries from many agencies. At that time the pastor was an American missionary, Dr Spahr, who trained pastors and leaders. On Sunday evening we attended an evangelistic meeting at San Juan Gospel Hall to hear a Filipino preach in Tagalog, but sadly I recognized only a few words.

When we first arrived at the mission house, two missionaries, Russell Reed and Neville Cooper, were found to be suffering from typhoid fever, and were housed in a small building behind the home. They were in quarantine. I took over the responsibility of caring for them.

When the other Tagalog students went to Calapan to the sub-language school, I stayed a few more days to take care of my patients. I was invited to speak at the Businessmen's Christian Fellowship and was told I would need to wear either a suit and tie or the Filipino barong tagalog.

I went to a tailor close to the mission home and had a barong tagalog made for me for this occasion, but also used it regularly for years after that. The barong, an embroidered formal shirt, is made of pineapple fiber with hand-sewn decorations. It was considered full dress, and I didn't need a jacket or a tie.

After about ten days, Russell Reed recovered and was able to join his wife and children, who were on a ship in Manila Bay waiting to go home on furlough. The other missionary, Neville Cooper, returned to Mindoro to continue work with various language-groups.

With Neville and Russell out of quarantine, it was time for me to travel to Mindoro. My traveling companions were the two children of Alfie and May Johnson, Irish OMFers based in Calapan but running a literature distribution ministry throughout the country.

We boarded the open bus at Batangas pier, and I sat on a wooden bench. Under the bus was the luggage, including pigs, chickens, and other merchandise. The bus conductor, hanging on to the side of the bus, asked everyone where they were going. After some time, he returned and gave everyone a ticket. About half an hour later he collected money, and after another long wait returned the correct change to everyone. When there were no seats available in the bus, people stood on the side of the bus and hung on.

As the bus traveled through the villages, people with baskets of food jumped onto the side of the bus and offered roasted corn cobs, peanut brittle, and the Filipino delicacy, boiled balut—duck eggs 15 days toward hatching. The fertilized egg already has beak and feathers, and I never acquired a taste for this particular treat.

At Batangas pier, we got off the bus and onto a jeep going to Bauan, where a new OMF team was starting a church-planting ministry. Mr Cenit, leader of the Philippine Missionary Fellowship, preached every night on the beach as fishermen prepared their boats and nets for a night of fishing. There were a few benches and many people sat on the sand.

After an introduction, a Tagalog evangelistic film was shown and then Mr Cenit preached an evangelistic message. We were there for only one night, but we heard that after a long series of messages Mr Cenit finally gave an altar call and many people made a decision to follow Christ. This became the nucleus of a new church there.

***

The large, unpainted Calapan mission home at that time was a nice house with electricity, running water and toilets. The grass "roofs" of a coconut plantation lined the street. Necy Goco, the language teacher, came daily and we each had a private lesson. We also had a group class with her in the mornings.

In the afternoons we visited Filipinos to practice what we had learned. On Sundays we usually attended the United Church of Christ in the Philippines. Theophilus Tolentino was the pastor. We had opportunities to speak at the youth fellowship. When I was introduced to the youth group, I found on the church bulletin: "Mr Tomb will speak today."

One weekend Theophilus took me to a preaching point out in the countryside. He asked me to speak in English, and he interpreted for me.

At the end of the weekend I asked, "Why, after months of Tagalog study, can I understand only an occasional word?"

He explained that we were in an Ilocano village and the people didn't speak Tagalog.

For Christmas, Dr Rudolfo Pareno, pastor of Grace Church in Manila, brought a group of students to visit the mountainous area where indigenous peoples lived. I had the privilege of going with them. We went to the village of Bayanan where we witnessed the baptism of 12 people in the river that flowed around the village. Then we went to a little chapel and celebrated the Lord's Supper. The preaching was on 1 Corinthians 3.9 (NKJV), "For we are God's fellow workers; you are God's field, you are God's building." His message was well illustrated from the agricultural practices of the Mangyan people.

When the church service was done, we climbed up the hill, heading to the village of Ayan Bekeg to visit some Christians there. It took us two hours to reach this Alangan congregation, whose members still used mainly Tagalog in their services. For meals and sleeping we were assigned to different homes around the village. Rice was served on a banana leaf, and a student from Manila brought a sauce composed of fish mixed with salt till it became a liquid, called bagoong. I found it very difficult to eat rice without salt or vegetables, but this was an introduction to life among the indigenous people-groups.

During this conference Akingan, one of the church leaders, asked about his son who had died. Near the village the people had set up pig traps, and all the children were warned not to go near this area. Akingan's son had disobeyed and had been shot through the stomach with a poisoned arrow.

"Is my son in heaven?" he asked. "He hasn't memorized all the Bible verses yet."

This conversation introduced us to local life and customs. It also gave us students the opportunity to explain the gospel and comfort the parents.

"Yes," I told the father. "It is important to memorize verses from the Bible, but we are all saved by the grace of God, not our own efforts."

After completing the second section of the Tagalog language curriculum, there was a test. My task was to teach a children's class. Our language coordinator and a high-school student came with me. We found a suitable spot and beckoned to some children to come listen. It was possible to gather a group of children at any time in any place in the Philippines. The language coordinator evaluated my feeble efforts. She generously gave me a passing grade so I could start the next section of language study.

***

After I had been studying Tagalog for several months in Calapan, Pastor Esteban Cruz requested that OMF missionaries help him in his church-planting ministry, so we joined him. A Christian owner of a hacienda had built a church building on the edge of his property, close to the road leading into Bongabon. He had also built a house for Pastor Cruz beside the church, and another house for the missionary Marie Barham and her co-workers. (Marie Barham had been a missionary in China with the

China Inland Mission, but had to leave China in the early 1950s. It was then she came to the Philippines and worked with the northern people-groups.) The owner asked Pastor Cruz to stay, evangelize the people working for him, and plant a church. Pastor Cruz also arranged for one of the young women from his congregation to teach my friend Nick and me Tagalog.

When we went to our tutor's house her cousin was always there as chaperone. He humorously played love songs on his guitar and serenaded us as we attempted to learn the language.

In the Philippine culture a companion is very important, and everyone would ask us single men, "Who is your *kasama*, your companion?"

When my single friends and I told them we had no companions they would ask, "Where is your mother? Why are you here without your mother to take care of you?"

Filipino men do not cook, so our landlady taught us very carefully how to cook Filipino food. Early each morning we went to the market to buy fresh vegetables and meat. Nick insisted that we needed to get used to Filipino food, so we didn't buy any bread.

As we walked back from the market, we heard children walking down the street shouting, "*Bili na kayo tinapay?* Will you buy some bread?"

Sometimes we heard, "*Americano, bili na kayo tinapay?* Americans, will you buy some bread?"

Actually the morning pan de sal, salt bread, was very tasty and eaten by most Filipinos every morning. Up in the mountainous areas of the rainforest the indigenous peoples didn't have bread, but they also bought bread when they went to town. My hope was still that I would live up in the bush among them someday.

8

Mindoro
1957

When Russell and Barbara Reed returned from their first furlough, they weren't sure about their welcome back to work with the Occidental Tawbuhid people. During their first term they had lived at Ligaya, a little village halfway down the west coast of Mindoro, and walked inland to the Tawbuhid village several times each week. They had left their things in their rented base-house in the village of Ligaya. I was asked to go with Russell to see how things were and if the people they had known were still in the area where they had previously met them. Russell and I took a ship from Manila to Ligaya.

We found everything still in the house. We walked out to the area where some of the Tawbuhid people lived and, after several wrong turns, through thick bamboo plantations, we found the same group, sitting around a campfire. We sat on the grass nearby. Russell talked to them, as they sat with their backs to him. He asked about all the people in the group who were not present. From what I remember, one had died a natural death, and another had been poisoned. It seemed a very lukewarm response to me. However, Russell decided to return to this village with his family.

I was challenged by his willingness to return to work with these people who had given him what seemed to me a cold reception. But the Mangyan, one of the people-groups of Mindoro, are not demonstrative and do not show their excitement openly. What seemed a chilly welcome might have been as warm as they come.

After our visit to Ligaya, we found there were no ships going back to Manila in the near future so we walked along the sand on the seashore. At every little shop along the way we bought one soft drink, usually

65

warm, but at least it gave us liquid. As it started to get dark, we reached a big river. We attempted to ford it at several points but it was too deep.

We found a man with a boat who offered to take us to his house on an island in the middle of the river, and to take us to the other side of the river in the morning, so we accepted his offer.

His house was a typical rural dwelling with one room in which everyone slept together. The parents slept in the middle, with the boys on the father's side and the girls on the mother's side of the room. There was a little kitchen in a semi-detached lower room which Filipinos describe as "outside." In the morning the women cooked breakfast and served the men first, according to the Filipino custom. We had rice and eggs. Russell looked at all the children the family had to care for and thought we should leave the eggs for them, but when he suggested this to the hostess she responded, "So your religion forbids you to eat eggs?"

Next morning we continued our trip, walking most of the day, and eventually reached Mamburao, the capital of Occidental Mindoro. There was a home for missionaries working in Mamburao. We had showers there and Russell waited for a boat to Manila, so that he could go and bring his family back to Ligaya. I got a jeep going to a town on the west coast called Paluan.

Dave Fuller and Bob Samms were missionaries in Paluan. Dave was on vacation in Baguio at the time, so I was assigned to stay with Bob for a couple of weeks. We had a good time together there as we walked into the bush to meet with the Iraya people, among whom Dave had just started a ministry. After a couple of weeks with Bob Samms, I returned to Bongabon.

In Bongabon, Pastor Cruz helped us students to be established in two churches. On Wednesday evenings, he often asked me to speak, but when I was finished he would say, "*Ang ibig niyang sabihin . . .* The thing he wanted to say was . . ." And then he would preach his own message. Sometimes this message was something I would never have taught.

One church in town was used for Eric Liberty's evangelistic meetings, which Pastor Cruz interpreted. OMF did not supply buildings for local churches, so this site was intended only for the evangelistic meetings.

Shortly after we arrived in Bongabon, this building had to be moved from one lot to another. Workmen with carabaos—water buffalos—came to move it, and we did some clean-up. Later that night the wives of these workmen came to ask for some money from all the believers. I asked our landlady how much we should give.

The landlady approached the wives. "These Americanos are very poor," she told them. "They even eat *kangkong*."

Kangkong was a vegetable which grew wild in the swamps. And the landlady was right. We did eat that! So in the end the women refused to take any money from us. Other families in the church gave them something, and the church gave them a donation.

We soon started children's meetings and offered Bibles to those who memorized a set number of verses. Our class may not have been very good, but it was popular with the little children. Each lesson was prepared and gone over with the help of our language teacher. When the children could say correctly a list of 12 verses, they got a Gospel of John. After they had memorized a second list of verses, they got a New Testament. A few even learned a third list of verses and got a whole Bible, which was a thick tome.

Neville Cooper took us to visit a church in an area where he was working on the Batangan River, where some Buhid people lived. This group had been almost wiped out by smallpox a number of years earlier, but a priest vaccinated a number of children, who survived. These people spoke the same language as the Buhid on the Apnagan River, but they didn't know the ancient writing, which was done with the point of a bolo, a long knife, on pieces of wood, mostly made of bamboo sticks. The form of the language represented the consonants of the words without necessarily the vowels, and was too inexact for a good Bible translation.

Marie Barham had also started a ministry in this area. Marie got cancer and died before she saw anyone turning to the Lord, but she worked intensively with Chief Lisigan, one of the local leaders. A film was produced about the Mangyan tribes, with a very poignant section about Marie Barham's life, work and death. I had shown this film many times when I was in Scotland, and now here I was, working with the same people.

One of the Filipino Christians was an enterprising young man, newly married, named Daganay. He had invited the missionaries to come and live at his place. He was even building a house for the missionaries next door. People walking up and down the riverside were invited to hear the gospel. Meetings started within his home, and he later built a chapel.

Before arriving at Daganay's house, the Buhid stopped at the river and bathed, and came dripping wet to the Sunday morning service. They had very few clothes, and soon dried off.

Neville Cooper had barely started his sermon when Daganay said, "Let's pray." One after another the people prayed. Some prayed their own prayers, some repeated what someone else had said, and some merely suggested what to pray for. Then they all prayed together at the same time. Neville explained that the Buhid classified those who prayed their own prayers as believers, those who repeated someone else's prayer as seekers, and those who didn't pray as unbelievers.

Frances Williamson—whom we had met in Singapore and who had brought us to the Philippines—was working with Fay Goddard with the Buhid people on the Apnagan River. They were always with the Buhid on Sundays, so whenever we preached at the hacienda church we were welcome to cook lunch and have an after-lunch siesta at their house before returning to town.

Frances and Fay took us to the Apnagan River to visit the people they were serving. One lady in the village told us that, at one time or another, she had been the wife of each man in the village. Some came to believe that the men exchanged wives every harvest time.

Many Buhid people who came from the interior had a disease called yaws. They had large sores on their skin, which often penetrated to muscle and bone. Frances had ordered supplies of medicine because she knew about the needs of the people in the remote areas. I brought the medicine in and started giving out two shots of penicillin, 12 hours apart, and soon they were completely cured. This established me as a miracle worker!

During the time I was in Bongabon, I made several trips to the villagers in the bush, sometimes with the missionaries who worked there and a few times without them, to give medicines to their sick people. I treated a man with many open sores, and stiff joints which did not bend. After I treated him, he walked with me over some very steep hills back to the main village. He climbed those hills more easily than I did with two healthy legs.

A few months later, I was asked to go with Fay Goddard to Manila because she had suddenly fallen ill. Anyone with a diagnosed disease could not fly on the local Philippine Airlines flight, but with her disease unknown it was possible to carry her into the plane.

When we arrived at Manila airport an ambulance was waiting for her and she was taken directly to a hospital, where she was diagnosed with polio. She was put on life-support equipment and flown back to the USA on a military plane. Fay was the second OMFer on Mindoro to get polio. After treatment, when she was no longer in an iron lung, she did editorial and art work for the OMF magazine *The Millions* from her wheelchair.

In Kaagutayan and Bayanan the group of believers grew. By this time the Far East Broadcasting Company had developed "portable missionaries," which were radios pre-tuned to the Christian radio station DZAS. They could pick up DZAS and nothing else.

Before this time, the first group to attempt to evangelize these people was a team from Gospel Recordings, who had recorded translations of Bible verses, stories and songs, and made these into phonograph records. The records, with hand-wound players, were distributed to anyone willing to use them. These early players only worked while someone was turning the handle, which meant that at least one person was listening.

The newest "portable missionaries" were just barely portable, working from a heavy car battery which had to be taken periodically to Manila to be recharged. The people listened very carefully to the radio, and whatever the radio said was regarded as true, although what the missionaries said was sometimes questioned.

The programs included news, health and agricultural tips, and both devotional and evangelistic messages. What the people heard of radio programs, particularly at Kaagutayan, set the form of their church meetings. Everything that was announced was stated as, "The next item on our program is . . ." Then, before reading the Scriptures, Pastor Angel, a villager who had previously been a spirit medium, would say, "Now we come to the sweetest part of our program, the reading of God's word." Finally, when he came to the end of the church service he would say, "Thank you very much for listening. Come again tomorrow at the same time." He preached the gospel every night to whoever was in his house.

The local believers had special classes with instructions about becoming a church. All who wanted to be baptized were publicly examined as to their faith and lives. The leadership made a big issue of chewing betel nut, so baptismal candidates were always asked, "How long is it since you stopped chewing betel nut?"

This practice involved chewing a mixture of tobacco, lime, and a piece of a specific nut that deadened the pain which many people had due to poor teeth. The early missionaries emphasized the need to quit chewing betel nut due to its addictive properties. The concern was that addiction to the narcotic took focus off the Lordship of Christ and obedience to him, but not everyone believed this was necessary. At the time, the custom when meeting people along the trail through the bush was to stop and exchange some leaves or lime and chew betel nut while talking, so this custom was used by some as an evangelistic opportunity.

Other questions the local people were required to answer were, "Do you know everything about God?", to which they were to answer "Yes." And "Are you afraid to die?" to which they were to answer "No." The villages of Kaagutayan and Bayanan were each close to a river, so the people who were accepted by the group were baptized.

Every year all the OMF missionaries met together for several days for a "field conference." My first few conferences were at the vacation home at Baguio, in the cool mountains on the island of Luzon. For these conferences there was always a special speaker, usually one of the mission directors from Singapore.

At the conference, people were elected to certain offices and assigned special jobs to do for the group. We also went regularly to Baguio for a vacation, and we had to schedule our time there. Families with children in the mission's boarding school had first choice of vacation dates. In Baguio we saw colorful indigenous people very different from the Mangyan among whom we lived. In the cooler climate many vegetables and fruit were available which we could not get elsewhere, so we enjoyed the fresh produce there.

One man from the remote mountainous areas, Palay Barsogon, was related to some people at Ayan Bekeg. He made a number of visits there, heard the gospel, received Jesus as Savior, and was baptized at Ayan Bekeg with some of the other Alangan believers. He participated with others in building a chapel and during that whole day did not chew betel nut, and decided that if he could go all day without it he could quit. Palay lived in the village of Magdangga, about three hours' walk into the hills (a hike of about seven hours for me). He witnessed to people in several other villages in the interior.

While I was still working in Bongabon, Palay Barsogon approached our superintendent, Dr Broomhall.

"There are several missionaries in villages at the foot of the hills," he said. "Can someone come to my village and teach us too?"

Dr Broomhall asked me if I would do this, so I was assigned to work with Palay. I moved back to Calapan, where I had my base. My assignment was to teach and live mostly at Comunal and take trips with Palay to Magdangga and other villages on alternate weeks. I was to go to Comunal on a Friday, stay for a week to teach the children after school, and Palay would come for me a week later.

The evening before going to Comunal, I read 2 Chronicles 20 (paraphrased): "Do not be afraid or discouraged . . . Stand firm and see the deliverance of the Lord. Tomorrow go down. The Lord will be with you."

With the encouragement of the Scriptures, I took the first bus in the morning to Santa Rosa. It was a bumpy road and I was lurching to and fro as I peered out the open sides. Frances Williamson came from San Teodoro and met me at the Santa Rosa bus stop. I was travel-stained, and wiped at the dirt and grit on my face as we walked to the home of the Reyes family, who lived beside the Alag River. Mr Reyes was the "barrio captain"—village leader. He took us across the river in his dug-out canoe.

Frances introduced me to the leading people in the village of Comunal, which was on the other side of the river from the Reyes' home. She showed me where things were in the house the people had built for her several years before.

I accompanied Frances as far as the river, taking a bucket with me to fetch water. Mr Reyes was waiting to take her back across the river, and from there she walked back to Santa Rosa for her bus. When I got back to the house, everything seemed very quiet. I walked around the village, but found it deserted. All the people had gone to the hills, to their fields. They didn't come back the entire week, because they were afraid of me. I waited there for a whole seven days, but no one returned to the village. At the end of the week, as arranged, Palay and his younger brother Ninardo came to accompany me to their village.

For a long time the people of Comunal did not return to the village from the rainforest where they lived. The school at Comunal had a Filipino teacher who came to the village for a week at a time to teach the children from those remote areas, but neither the teacher nor the students were there regularly. I visited Comunal several times but always found the village deserted. After a few weeks there was a big typhoon, which blew down many trees and destroyed many houses. The house built for another missionary, Marguerite Furer, was broken down during a typhoon when a huge banana plant fell on the roof. I was able to rescue the medical equipment, but most of the other things in the house had already disappeared. On my way to the interior with Palay I often went through Comunal, but no one in the village wanted to study the Bible with me. After so long I was available and prepared. But had all my preparation been for nothing?

9

Villages of the rainforest
1959–1961

The hillside rose above me, and the sun's hot rays hit my shoulders. I lifted my arm and wiped the sweat from my brow. Blinking my eyes, I focused on the next stepping stone. How much time had passed? I wasn't sure, but glancing up, it seemed we couldn't be more than halfway up the mountain. Palay, my guide, paused before me, no doubt sensing my weariness. He motioned for us to pause, and I gladly sat down to rest.

Palay was the oldest of three brothers. The younger two were Ninardo and Manuel. Palay had told me his father was dead, but I later discovered he meant spiritually dead, an unbeliever living in Magdangga. Palay's wife Reganium had had five babies who all died at birth or soon after. Then, finally, they had a girl who survived and grew up.

Palay and Ninardo had placed the stepping stones up the hills to make the trail easier. Now as we rested, Palay untied a package wrapped in a banana leaf. He smiled and opened it to show me.

My stomach growled. Boiled sweet potatoes.

"From Reganium," he said. "To give you strength for the climb."

I took one in my hand and took a bite. As I ate, my strength returned. Before long, we continued upward, but not to Magdangga, as I had expected. Instead, I found myself in a village called Badyang.

"Many families want you to teach," Palay explained. "They have heard only a little of the gospel but have become Christians."

"You're a good witness, Palay." I placed my hand on his shoulder and scanned the area. The small village had been constructed on a flat piece of land.

Palay pointed to a two-level house. The slightly raised area was where I would sleep, and the lower area where I could teach a class. Other houses were set out in a circle on the flat plateau, all built up on stilts due to

73

possible flooding from the river and for protection from animals. The only building not on stilts was the chapel, which had benches at ground level.

Every morning I gathered with the people in the little chapel for Bible study, prayer and singing. Then, with hearts full of worship, the adults hurried to their fields to work for the day. The children stayed to study reading and writing. Happy chatter filled the air as they went about their work.

After dark, the adults returned from the fields and ate—often their only meal of the day. Then, I would open the Bible before them to teach. The only time I didn't teach was when I visited other villages with Palay or another guide. Over time it became a pattern to stay two weeks at a time at Badyang, leave to teach, and then return, making sure to be there on Sunday. Twelve adults soon asked to be baptized, and their decision nourished me even more than sweet potatoes during a long climb.

When I taught about the Lord's Supper, the villagers asked, "How can Mangyan become Christians? We don't have any bread, and grapes don't grow here."

We went back to the Gospels, and I read the account of the Lord eating the last supper.

"Look here," I told them. "Jesus took things that were on the table and gave them special meaning. We can take whatever we have on our table to eat, and use it."

The same sort of question came up with the offering. The people would say, "We don't have any money here in the hills. We can only get money by going to work for farmers in the lowlands."

We read through every Scripture verse I could find about money without comment.

A few days later they asked me, "Do you have an old can?"

I gave them an empty margarine container. The next Sunday this was passed from one to the other, and they found that they did have something to give.

When we set the date for the baptism, I invited Hazel Page and a newly arrived missionary from Australia to join me. Hazel Page from OMF was the language coordinator for indigenous languages. She had started with Wycliffe in Mexico teaching literacy, was unable to get into China, and instead focused on several of the minority Mexican languages. Hazel went to China when it opened up, and did literacy work there with smaller ethnic groups. When that door closed, she turned to the Philippines.

A couple of elders from the church at Ayan Bekeg came to do the baptizing at Badyang. We arrived and found that the little brook running close to the village had not yet been dammed up as the people had promised, so there was no water deep enough for baptism by immersion. The first thing we had to do, therefore, was to build a dam. Then we had an examination of the baptismal candidates.

The next morning enough water had collected above our dam to allow us to kneel down and go under the water forward. Two of the elders from the church at Ayan Bekeg baptized the believers who had been examined the previous day. After the baptism we met in the chapel and for the first time in that village "broke bread," but it was a unique experience, especially for us expats. We used a sweet potato for bread, and then each of us found a small leaf, which we folded into the shape of a cup. Water was poured into all the cups, and we used the water to symbolize the blood of Jesus shed for the remission of sin.

With Palay and the local preacher from the village of Bayanan, I took many trips into the hills. Palay was so deficient in good nourishment that he needed a couple of weeks to recover from a trip, so the two men alternated. Many of the indigenous people were malnourished as this was a time of famine brought on by lack of rain.

I went to one village with Palay, and as we came over the ridge and looked down on the village, we saw the people cooking in their houses. It had taken us all day to get there, mainly because I had slipped so often on the muddy trail, and we had all needed rest times to get rid of the leeches that climbed up our legs and sucked our blood. Then, as we watched, we saw the families leave their houses, and the village was soon deserted.

We spent the night in the home of Palay's uncle, ate the food we had brought for our dinner, had our own Bible study, and having seen no one by morning, we left to return to Badyang.

On one of these trips, I was with a young man going up a very steep muddy trail with a precipice on the side of the hill. Every time I slipped he would say, "*Salamat Panginoon!* Thank you, Lord!"

"Why do you say that?" I finally asked him.

"I thank the Lord that you didn't slip all the way down this mountain. If you landed in that gully, I would never be able to get you out."

Amazingly, the hazardous trips up and down the mountains weren't the biggest concern for me. Instead, the more I worked with the remote people-groups, the more I considered my need for a wife.

When I started visiting the villages deep in the mountains of Mindoro, I understood that among the peoples of the interior, a male missionary most needed a woman by his side. First, because much of my day was spent doing tasks like cooking and hauling water. I could see how having a wife who was willing to take on these hard but essential tasks would free me to do more evangelism work.

Second, while we were discussing the biblical need for an elder to be the husband of one wife, Palay's younger brother Ninardo explained that in their culture a single man could acceptably function as an elder while still living in his parents' home, but a male evangelist going from village to village needed to be married because people wouldn't believe his explanation. They would believe that he was coming to their village only to look for a wife.

During my first year as a missionary, when I returned from one of my trips into the rainforest, there was a new language-group in Calapan with several young ladies. I was only in Calapan a couple of days, preparing for my next trip.

One young missionary nurse stood out to me the most. Her name was Caroline. She was a missionary from the United States and had beautiful blonde curls. She had made the most wonderful cinnamon rolls, which we all enjoyed. Also, she had arrived in the Philippines with a piano accordion. Caroline seemed like someone who would make a good companion, and her music could help with church planting.

Yet even though I found myself thinking about her often and wanting to see her, I was conflicted. As I lay in bed imagining how nice it would be to have a companion like Caroline, I thought back to my days at Bible school in Glasgow. The director of OMF had visited us and preached. His words played through my mind: "In OMF we need single young men to scale the hills and go to far-off places."

Taking on the calling of a missionary, I had resigned myself to doing without romance, food, support, and other "rights" that I had given up for the sake of the gospel. I had come to the Philippines expecting to be permanently single, yet I found that even washing clothes or fetching water was socially unacceptable for men to do. Also, these things took all day in the rainforest, stripping time from my evangelistic work.

Over the months, my attitude changed. Having a wife had become a need—I needed a wife to have enough assistance to do my missionary work. And even though I had once closed my heart to relationships—after losing so many people I had loved—my heart started to open. A marriage partner would complete my work in ways I hadn't anticipated when I set off for the mission field. Caroline—a good cook and musician—seemed an excellent fit for ministry . . . and for my heart.

After dinner one night I asked Caroline if I could speak with her when she came for evening refreshments. I thought she had said yes, but she didn't show up. Because I was going back to the mountains on the first bus in the morning, I wrote her a letter of proposal. She replied, and I realized she hadn't been thinking about me as much as I had been thinking about her. Caroline was not interested in marriage, and she suggested someone else.

Caroline's side of this story is different. She doesn't recall my asking to speak with her, and remembers getting my letter out of the blue.

After completing language study in Calapan, Caroline was assigned to work with Frances Williamson in San Teodoro and Kaagutayan. I made a point of visiting the church at Kaagutayan frequently between other trips, so I could see her.

I was caught up in extreme weather a couple of times at San Teodoro. On one occasion I was sleeping at the home of Jose, an older single man from the San Teodoro church, when a typhoon hit and blew off the metal sheet covering the ridge of the thatched roof. The rain poured into the house. We both looked for a dry spot. I found a closet where bedding was kept during the day, and slept there for the rest of the night.

***

Another village I frequently visited was Albigayan. One of the young girls from there had gone to Bayanan regularly, heard the gospel, and received Jesus Christ as Savior. She tried hard to teach the children and others in her village, but they weren't very receptive. Hazel Page visited, and the villagers built a house for her. I went there with one of the older boys from my literacy class to help.

One day, on the way back to Badyang from Albigayan, my guide insisted on visiting a house on the way. We sat near the door, and soon other people started arriving. The lady of the house pulled the big pot off the fire and cut the pieces of meat into smaller chunks. Soon we were all served sweet potatoes and monkey soup, with chunks of monkey meat very deliciously cooked.

One of the older men of Albigayan lived in a house directly in front of my house, so when I arrived and had set up my few belongings, I went across to see him. His house was full of people visiting.

After some time, the old man approached me. "*Kaibigan*, friend, what do you eat?"

I had been taught, when approaching a new community, to eat what the indigenous people ate. So I replied politely, "I'll eat what you are eating."

We went on talking for some time, and then I smelt something like fur burning.

The old man turned to me. "*Kaibigan*, today we are eating rat. Will you pray before we eat?"

I prayed quietly to myself, asking God to help me eat some of the things offered. As one missionary put it: "Lord, I'll swallow this, but you've got to help me keep it down!" As it turned out, I was amazed how tender and tasty the rat was. It was one of the easier things to digest. I had also learned to eat mice, wild cat, snakes, bugs, slugs, roasted worms, immature bees, boiled leaves—including leaves like elephant ears that made your throat pucker up—wild tomatoes, squash, rice, sweet potatoes of various kinds, poisonous roots that were cut in slices, soaked three times and dried to remove the poison, and many other things.

Between trips to other places with Palay and another Filipino Christian, named Carding Bulaklak, I often visited Albigayan for a week or so at a time. One Sunday morning I felt particularly cold, but still went to the house where we were going to have Sunday worship. I didn't know what was wrong with me, but I was shivering. I led the morning service and doggedly gave the message I had prepared, but my body was shaking so hard that the whole house quivered.

After the service, I lay for a short time in front of a big fire. With urging from the old man—and the promise of a *kasama* (companion) along the trail down the hill—I set out. Soon I found that they had sent two teenaged girls to see I got to Bayanan safely.

Carding saw me at Bayanan and accompanied me to the bus stop, a couple of hours' walk away. When we got to the river his eyes narrowed in concern.

"With a fever like you have," he said, "you shouldn't wade through the water. Let me carry you."

But I insisted on wading through the river, while he held me up.

Back at the mission home in Calapan, I found that I had an infection in my leg, probably caused by walking through the bush in shorts and getting scratched, then wading through dirty water. I took a course of antibiotics, and then returned to my work of visiting the remote villages in the hills. I frequently had these infections: they were almost unavoidable.

One day I was in Calapan, taking an antibiotic for another leg infection, when Dr Broomhall received a letter from the south of the island. Missionaries Hazel Page and Elli Van der Linden had a number of Hanonoo believers who wanted to be baptized. I immediately got ready and took the bus to Mansalay, the base out of which the missionaries to the Hanonoo worked. By the time I got there they had already left, but I was invited to stay the night at their house, and the owner of their house offered to take me to Sinariri, the first Hanonoo village, where the missionaries were.

The next day I arrived and found about a dozen people wanting to be baptized. There was one man who had been baptized by the New Tribes Mission. With his participation I baptized another man, and then these two baptized the others. The missionaries gave me a translation of 1 Corinthians 11, and I conducted my first Lord's Supper in a mixture of Hanonoo and Tagalog. Hazel Page wanted me to speak in English, saying she could translate, but the people generously insisted they could under-stand my Tagalog.

On this trip I visited the three villages where the Hanonoo believers lived. At Turubong I was impressed with the forceful way in which some of these men answered the questions put to them by the congregation. I did not understand the words, but the way they answered was very clear. It was a thrilling opportunity for me.

When I returned to the Iraya work, I visited Pastor Angel and his wife Rosario at Kaagutayan. I told them how thrilled I was with the Hanonoo believers.

Rosario narrowed her gaze at me. "Have they stopped chewing betel nut?"

I smiled. "No, but they love Jesus!"

Although OMF was looking for single men to take the gospel to the remote people-groups scattered over the mountains, most of the missionaries who arrived in Mindoro were young women. It turned out that it was much easier for the timid forest-dwelling people to accept these ladies.

This also meant that even though the men could visit many places, it was necessary to be very careful that they didn't stay in houses where single ladies were staying. Filipinos were also suspicious if an equal number of men and women traveled together.

I had many opportunities to visit other missionaries and help them, but very few opportunities to have anyone join me in my work. Werner Demand, from Germany, and Don Byrne from Australia were about the only ones who came to visit me.

As one of the few male missionaries on the team, I was invited to baptize believers at Pambuhan, in the Abra de Ilog area and Hanonoo. Yet, in general, the people who lived in the rainforest were afraid that men were going to take their children to America to become soldiers. In practice, "the man for the job" was often a woman.

With Carding I went to the very center of the island, where he had relatives. We found a typical "long house," which is more common in Borneo than in Mindoro. In this huge building there were numerous fireplaces, and at night there was a family around each fire. Everyone was related, and often children slept with other families rather than their own.

It was corn-harvest time. The people went out into their field, picked as many ears of corn as they could carry, brought them home, and ate boiled corn on the cob. One day they found one or two monkeys stealing their corn, so they killed the monkeys, brought the bodies home, and cooked them for dinner.

Thomas at eight months old, living
at his grandmother's house in Brno,
Czechoslovakia.

Thomas on his father's lap. His father took
his own life while being hunted down by the
Nazis for deportation to a concentration camp.

Thomas's grandmother's house before the Second World War. Members of the household
staff are posing in the photo.

Thomas with Tony as children during happier times. Tony's life was taken from him in the Sosibór death camp.

Thomas's class in Těšany, Czechoslovakia. Thomas is in the top row, third from right. Thomas's mother insisted he take Christian instruction with the other students in his class.

Thomas with his mother Františka, called Franzi, and Tony at the fish pond near the large estate in Těšany, Czechoslovakia.

Thomas's travel document for the Kindertransport. This document was filed under his stepfather's last name, Hochberg, and Thomas insisted it be changed to his father's last name, Graumann.

Thomas and Tom Schlesinger with Miss Corson and her parrot Polly. Miss Corson initially offered to open her home to girls from the Kindertransport and then agreed to allow boys to come.

Thomas, aged 17, with Miss Corson who cared for him until adulthood.

Thomas as a student leader in Oban,
Scotland. His desire was to become an
overseas missionary.

Thomas's friend Daganay hearing the gospel for the first time on a
phonograph in 1959.

Thomas and Caroline on their wedding day, August 15, 1962.

Thomas and Caroline in their first Filipino home as a married couple.

Thomas and Caroline with their children Dan, Tim, Paul and Lyn. Thomas and Caroline had hopes of returning to the Philippines as missionaries with their children.

Thomas and Caroline with a class of Czech students they taught during their "retirement" years.

Thomas finally meets Nicholas Winton, the man who saved his life and the lives of 668 other children.

Thomas and Caroline with most of their children and grandchildren.

Every evening we held Bible studies, but they weren't interested. It was time to go, to move on.

***

Exhaustion filled me, yet the voices of many people stirred me from my sleep. I rubbed my eyes and sat up. Then my eyes opened wider. Everyone was staring intently at me, and waiting with eagerness.

My friend Angel approached. "They have all come to hear the gospel. They've been waiting for you to awake."

I smiled at Angel. He had invited me to visit some of his relatives over the hill at Kamarong. It had taken us all day to get there. When we arrived I was exhausted, and fell asleep. But now the sleepiness left me, seeing the interest in these eager faces.

We spent several days there sharing the gospel. The headman, Paustino, was very interested. Different families from the valley came, a few at a time. We went over the message of salvation and played recordings of the Gospels for them.

With Paustino, we visited the homes of several families in the valley and also the next valley. Paustino invited me to come back, so I arranged to return in a month's time between other trips.

When I returned I found a house built for me. Not only that, but Paustino's family moved in with me to take care of me and to be there all the time for teaching. He had also built a little chapel in which to meet. Yet we never used the chapel. It was much nicer to gather in the big house they had built for me.

After several visits, Paustino asked if I could teach his people to read and write. We started study with just a pencil, paper, and small flashcards. Tagalog is a phonetic language so any one symbol is always pronounced in the same way. Paustino learned quickly. I spent a week with him, mostly working on reading.

A month later I returned with reading primers, and as I approached the village I could see letters of the alphabet written with charcoal on every tree. After another week of reading lessons, I had to go on another trip, but left a few books there for my next visit. When I came back I found that Paustino had taken my New Testament and had gone from house to house, showing off his skill and reading Scripture to every family in his area.

Kamarong was a long walk to the north shore of the island of Mindoro, between Puerto Galera and Abra de Ilog. I would often ride a bus from San Teodoro to Puerto Galera and then walk along the north shore till I reached Kamarong. I could also catch a morning flight from Calapan to Mamburao, take a bus to Abra de Ilog, and walk a shorter distance along the north coast.

Sometimes after a long visit to Kamarong, I walked to Abra de Ilog and took a boat to Batangas and visited the Tolivers, missionaries I had known previously, at Bauan before taking the ferry to Calapan. I left my Tagalog Bible and phonograph player with records at Kamarong.

In 1961 a terrible fear gripped people throughout the Philippines that the world was going to end, and many climbed up into the hills. This panic began with a hoax perpetrated by a Catholic group to get people to spend money on candles and other religious merchandise. Catholic churches sold specially blessed candles for people to light as a way to prevent the coming end. I went to Kamarong that weekend because this was the newest group of believers, and I asked if they were afraid like other Filipinos.

Paustino told me, "The rumors can't be true. The phonograph records say that no one knows the day or the hour of the end of the world."

It was thrilling to know that these new Christians trusted the promises of Scripture.

For one visit to Kamarong, Werner Demand, the German missionary, joined me. We were there just before harvest time. There was no food in the valley. For several days all we had was a cup of coffee once a day. I got sick again and had a high fever. When the people brought us some of their first-harvested rice, I wasn't able to eat it, but they had also caught and cooked a big white fish. This tasted so good.

The next morning Werner left early and walked along the shoreline till he reached Abra de Ilog, where May Roy and her team lived. She was a senior missionary on the west coast, and was fluent in Urdu. When she was tired, Urdu words appeared in her Tagalog. She had new mission-aries working with her and taught them to be respectful to one another and their various styles of cooking. May had a church in town and an outreach to "mobile" villages. When these villages moved so that the people could find new fields and food sources, May's team went with them.

May was able to assist Werner in hiring a motorboat. With their help I walked to the boat, and they took me to Abra de Ilog pier where there was a bus for Mamburao waiting for passengers.

At Mamburao I got a tricycle to take me to the mission home. A tricycle is a bicycle with a sidecar built for two passengers. Filipinos decorate these vehicles with colorful designs, and sometimes have motorcycles with sidecars, which will carry loads and as many Filipinos as can climb onto the tricycle.

At the mission home, Nick and Doreen Wehren were temporarily assigned to help with the town church. They had just had twin boys, and Doreen was working on learning Tagalog.

Nick got the malaria team to come visit me. The medics took some blood, and it tested positive for tertiary malaria, so they gave me a shot of some new antimalarial drug and made arrangements for me to fly to Manila. In Manila, I checked in at the Adventist hospital. I don't remember much of the hospital other than the meat substitute that they served with the rice. I was diagnosed there with hepatitis, not malaria, and returned to the Manila OMF mission home in a very weak state.

10

Caroline

1961

Very soon after returning to Manila, because of the state of my health, I was sent back to the UK on a ship with John Lockhart and his family. He had been working with the OMF literature department and for some time had run the vacation home in Baguio, so I had stayed at his place in Baguio on a number of trips.

On the way to the UK we had a week in Hong Kong where we changed ships, made a few purchases, and visited the literature work of OMF in Hong Kong. It was interesting to see a Chinese magazine being prepared. On squared paper, one Chinese symbol had to be put in each square, and the editors had to take a manuscript and make it fit into these squares.

While in Hong Kong, we went with a group of OMFers for a picnic near the border with China, and we saw the Chinese mainland beyond the foothills. The Lockharts had two young children who were very interested in watching the planes land and take off on the runway being built into the sea for Hong Kong International Airport. Chinese laborers, with a pole placed across their shoulders and a basket on each end, were digging earth from the foothills of a local mountain and using it to extend the runway. A number of planes came in to land but, on finding the runway too short, took off again, and after circling around Hong Kong made another attempt to land.

Big H-shaped high-rise tower blocks rose up around us, built for Chinese immigrants to Hong Kong. Shops filled the ground level, and the single-roomed apartments each housed a family of up to nine. On the roof was a school for the children living in that apartment building. The population of each building was about a thousand people. OMF missionaries held Bible classes in several of these rooftop schools.

My body ached and fever plagued me on the ship back to the UK, but thankfully I had had a good day in Singapore when we visited the OMF headquarters at Cluny Road. For four years, I had corresponded with one of my Chinese Sunday school kids. His family arranged for a banquet with a number of people from their Chinese church. The restaurant they chose served food from north China so most of the dishes had noodles, not rice.

When we reached London, I immediately checked in at Mildmay Mission Hospital, and was a guinea pig while the doctors ran tests. They found many things wrong with me: malaria, hepatitis, various kinds of worms, and stomach issues. The hospital was quite short-staffed. About 30 men were in my ward, so I had many opportunities to help my fellow patients.

While I was a patient in this hospital, I was allowed on Sunday mornings to attend Westminster Chapel where Dr Martin Lloyd-Jones preached regularly. Before I went to the Philippines he had been teaching from Ephesians 2 and when I returned he had reached Ephesians 6, doing a major series on "the wiles of the devil," which included a study of the major cults of that time.

My first Sunday back was the day before the New English Bible was published. Dr Lloyd-Jones was convinced that one of the wiles of the devil was to have believers compare different Bible translations instead of interacting with the text and applying the teaching of Scripture to their lives.

After I was discharged from the hospital, I spent a little time at the OMF mission home at Newington Green in London and met one of my fellow students, Jimmy Hui. Mr Welch, in the deputation department, arranged speaking engagements for me in the London area.

I then traveled to Connel and stayed with Miss Corson for a few weeks. The young people from Oban Christian Endeavor made arrangements for me to speak in a number of places in the surrounding villages, and Ruby Watt, who had a car, made herself responsible for my transport. Ruby was one of the members of the CE group in Oban. She became a nurse, and after Uncle Jimmie's first wife Christine passed away, he married Ruby.

While in Oban, I found a nice Celtic cross with a pretty stone and sent this to Caroline. We had been corresponding by letter as friends, but when Caroline received this cross, she thought she ought to at least pray about a possible relationship with me.

It wasn't long until I received another letter from her with great news.

"Yes, I will marry you," she stated simply.

Dr Broomhall announced our engagement, and Caroline left the Philippines for an early furlough.

I traveled to London to meet her. Her train from the cross-Channel ferry was delayed. I called the station a number of times and eventually went there to wait. It was 3 a.m. before we arrived at Jimmy Hui's house, where he and his family had a big Chinese dinner waiting for us.

It was Sunday, and after a little sleep we spent the day in London shopping for shoes for Caroline. Then we took an early flight from London to Edinburgh to speak at the Baptist church where Dr Graham Scroggie and Alan Redpath had been pastors. When our friends discovered that we had caught a plane on a Sunday they were very upset: "You shouldn't have broken the Sabbath."

We bought a used car and traveled around, speaking at a number of churches as arranged by a Scottish representative of OMF. We went to one church in Fifeshire, where the people have a distinctive accent. Caroline turned to me and asked, "What are they saying? I can't understand them."

We also spent time in Edinburgh, where I slept at Uncle Jimmie's house and Caroline at the home of one of his camp helpers.

The next adventure lay before us—and for me in particular: meeting Caroline's family! We left our car with Uncle Jimmie to sell, and were able to get a passage on the last ship across the Atlantic before Christmas—on the USS *United States*.

It was a rough crossing. Caroline was sick most of the way.

***

My cousin John and his wife Hilda met us at the pier and took us to their home just outside New York. On our first Sunday morning in the USA we attended their Quaker meeting. In discussion with Hilda she told us that it is possible for a Quaker to believe in the deity of Jesus, but that she had never met anyone who did. I later discovered this was not the case.

With John we went to Vineland, New Jersey, to visit his mother. By this time Uncle Arthur had divorced Aunt Emma and had returned to Vienna for his last years. We saw the old chicken farm they had run (due to a chicken disease they had been forced to quit their business). We then drove back to New York and spent Christmas with John and his family. They showed us a little of the city, including the United Nations building where John was working. We also visited the New York office of OMF where we were given a rail ticket to travel across the States.

We first went from New York to Philadelphia and spent a couple of days at the US headquarters of OMF. From there we went to Chicago, where we stayed with two OMF representatives, the Matthews, who had been among the last missionaries to be able to get out of China when Western missions were expelled by the Communists in 1953.

While we were in Chicago we got a call from Caroline's brother Marvin to say he was living and working at Galveston, Texas, and that we should take a train to Houston where he would meet us. We spent a couple of days in Chicago. It was cold, especially for us, having come from the Philippines. So it was wonderful that we were able to reroute our travel from Chicago to Houston on the way to California. We left Chicago at about 20 degrees Fahrenheit (–7 °C), wearing every coat and scarf we had, and got off the train all bundled up at Houston, Texas, where the temperature was around 80 degrees (27 °C). Marvin laughed at us so warmly dressed.

We had a nice two days with Marvin and family. From Houston we took a train to Winslow, Arizona, and enjoyed some time with Caroline's brother Bob and his wife Jeanie. They took us to see the Grand Canyon. From there we went to San Diego to spend two days with Caroline's sister Ruth and her husband Tom.

After this we traveled to San Jose where Mom and Pop Bergen picked us up, and we spent the rest of my time in the USA at their place. We got a warm welcome at Twin Lakes Baptist Church.

When it was time for me to return home, I got a flight to the Philippines in an old propeller-driven plane. The seats were very close to one another, so there was little leg space. Most of the passengers were Filipinos, and many were taking home rattan bags filled with gifts for their families. We stopped to refuel at Hawaii, Midway and another island, before arriving at Okinawa. Here we had to stay for the night in a hotel, at airline expense. This was my first introduction to Japanese culture. The next morning the flight took us to Taiwan to refuel, and eventually to Manila. I had experienced my first international flight. At this point in time, world travel changed from ocean liners to planes.

As we landed, I couldn't help but marvel that Caroline and I had spent the last few months with her family. The word evoked complex associations. There was my family of origin. The Scottish "family" who had taken me in and had trained and discipled me, sending me out to do the Lord's work. My cousin John, one of my last biological relatives. And Caroline's family, which would soon be mine. And now we were returning to our missionary and Filipino families. God had given so much to that young boy who had been placed on the train with a tag around his neck. And soon I would have a companion for life.

11
A promise of a family
1962–1966

The aroma of tropical flowers filled the air, and their beauty decorated the pulpit. Caroline and I stood next to each other in the nipa-leaf thatched building up in the hills. Friends from the local people-groups and fellow missionaries gathered around us. They also looked in from the outside. Pastor Esteban Cruz performed the wedding, though far from well. He wiped his feverish brow and insisted on being there, even though he should have been in bed.

The wedding included a teaching about marriage and a short message by Dr Broomhall. Then Caroline and I exchanged our vows and signed the certificate, dated August 15, 1962. Dr and Mrs Broomhall were our sponsors. There was a simple reception after the wedding with coffee made with brown sugar in Filipino style, brewed in a five-gallon drum and served with local cookies.

It felt good to have Caroline by my side, for good. The year before our wedding, she had spent the year of furlough in the USA and had undergone major ear surgery. She had been suffering from an ear infection that had persisted since she was five years old. The infection had been so bad as a child that her mother prayed to God for her life, and through that commitment her mother made to God, Caroline came to Christ also. Yet she had continued to have issues with that ear until about the age of 30. During our time apart, we corresponded frequently, planning our wedding by mail.

On visits to the villages in the rainforest, I had asked believers about their weddings and related customs. Parents traditionally arranged the marriages, and while there was no bride price, the groom had to work for the bride's family for a year. Among the Hanonoo the bride had to be able to spin thread, make clothes, and cook. The man had to build a house and create a field.

However, most of the church leaders told me that they had eloped with their brides, often taking the woman from another man, and after a "honeymoon" in the remote forested areas had returned to the village "married." Their new-found love gave them the passion to go against their families' previously arranged marriages for them. Then the couple went to the municipal offices in the town and obtained a legal marriage certificate, which they waved in front of their birth families. Parents were often angry as they had already made an arrangement for a union with a prestigious family. The new believers were interested in our understanding of Christian marriage and God's design for the family.

After our wedding in the mountain village, we walked to the bus stop, about two hours away, and took the bus into Calapan. On arrival we found the mission home decorated for the occasion. After a shower, Caroline went to a hairdresser, who initially piled her hair on top of her head, perhaps in the usual style for a Filipino wedding, but Caroline didn't like it. She requested a different hairstyle, which took a bit longer. She was still at the hairdresser when the Chinese restaurant delivered the wedding dinner, and the bakery brought the decorated wedding cake, which Caroline had baked the day before. One layer was a typical American white cake, with a British fruit cake for the lower layer.

After the dinner we had the wedding cake and exchange of rings, which we hadn't considered necessary to introduce into the service held in the mountains. The next morning, we went to the Calapan airport via a *calesa*, a horse-drawn carriage. We had our photos developed and had our wedding papers registered at the British and American embassies.

After this reception at the Manila mission home, which we had not expected, we went to Baguio, the vacation capital of the Philippines. Many missionaries, as well as Filipinos, enjoy the cool atmosphere high up in the mountains of Luzon Island. Fatigued bodies quickly gained new enthusiasm. We booked the "honeymoon cottage" of the ABWE mission.

During our honeymoon the Overseas Christian Servicemen's Centers held a conference. We went there one evening and enjoyed the meeting. Several of the servicemen gave refreshing testimonies. We also learned the song, "His Name Is Wonderful."

After a couple of weeks in the cool of Baguio, we returned to Mindoro. We set up our base at San Teodoro, a little town about 13 miles west of Calapan. There were buses several times a day along the partially paved road. Caroline had found this house before going home for furlough. The former occupants had kept chickens in the kitchen, and the walls were crawling with insects. Caroline sprayed the walls with disinfectant—but got hepatitis from the spray. A missionary doctor studying Tagalog in Calapan made the trip to San Teodoro to give her intravenous (IV) fluids.

From our base we visited the villages of Kaagutayan and Bayanan regularly, and made other trips. Our nicest indigenous-style house was at Bayanan. The floor was about five feet off the ground, with a strong ladder leading up to it. It had a doorway and window openings but no door or windows. The roof was made of cogon-leaf shingles, the walls were part rattan and part cogon shingles, and the floor was of split bamboo. The house had a separate bedroom. Our bed consisted of a thin foam mattress that covered the entire floor, and a double sleeping bag.

There was a kitchen with a table attached to the west wall and a pump pressure stove. Water came from the river in buckets and needed to be boiled and cooled for drinking. There was also an outer room with a bench and paraffin cans for storage. On the walls of the outer room we hung teaching posters, and provided books and other reading materials for people to look at while waiting there. The village children liked the *National Geographic* magazine. They used to play a little game: they would open the copy, and the first to place a hand on whatever he or she saw said "Mine!"

Caroline did the majority of the medical work, while I spent most of my time preparing teaching lessons and preaching. We trained a few older girls to be Sunday school teachers, using some of the teacher training courses prepared in Tagalog by Child Evangelism Fellowship.

We worked among the Iraya people, who were the most timid of all the indigenous groups of Mindoro. When they were afraid of someone, they would go and hide deep in the bush. They sometimes came into our house and sat quietly for half an hour before saying anything. Often as they were leaving they would ask, "Is there any medicine here? Can I have some?"

"What is wrong?" was my response. "Why do you need medicine?"

Before putting antibiotic ointment on a sore, we sent people to the river to wash first. They had customs about bathing. You shouldn't bathe when you are hot or when you are cold. You shouldn't bathe in the evening. We seemed to find lots of reasons to send them to bathe.

During the next four years we fought a continuing battle with scabies. We had people come to our house, bathe, and come back to plaster themselves with a paste made of an American washing detergent, available locally. This could clear up the scabies, but if the whole community didn't do it they reinfected one another.

In the remote mountainous areas, all missionaries did medical work. Those who didn't know much about medicines gave out aspirin and vitamins. Some of us with medical training tried to treat people more adequately. I spent many weeks going from one village to another giving shots of streptomycin and other medicines we were able to buy from Hong Kong without a prescription. When we gave out medicine we told patients what we were charging and left it up to them to bring us something in exchange. In this way they kept us supplied with rice, sweet potatoes and vegetables while we were in their isolated village.

Shortly after we were married, Caroline developed a very bad cough due to chronic bronchitis. In our medical supplies we had some penicillin in oil, which needed only one injection daily. I gave Caroline a series of penicillin injections in her buttocks. The cough didn't improve for a long time, and the penicillin remained in little lumps under her skin and was not absorbed. In due course we went to Manila, and Caroline had several minor operations to remove the lumps of penicillin. This was done over a period of time, so I went back to Mindoro for a while.

When I got back to Mindoro, I saw that our bank account was very depleted, and this concerned me. One day a letter arrived from a bank in Calapan. It said, "You have a hundred Australian dollars in your account here. It has been here for a year. What do you want to do with it?" We got word of this money just when we needed it.

I went back to Manila for Caroline's final operation. The hospital bed was not clean, and there were bugs crawling around. The anesthesiologist gave Caroline a spinal injection, and when she felt the numbness moving up her body she was scared. The wounds were left open to close up slowly, which left big scars, but the doctor hadn't cut deeply enough, so many of the lumps of penicillin remained deeper down in her buttocks. With nothing more that could be done, my brave wife returned to Mindoro and we continued with our work.

Although we worked mainly with the Iraya churches at Kaagutayan and Bayanan, we did a lot of traveling from village to village. One day as we were walking through the village of Santa Rosa to catch our bus, a young man invited us to have Sunday evening meetings at his house. He gathered a house-full of local people. Meetings continued at his house weekly for several months, but no one was ready to turn to the Lord and the initiative fizzled out.

As we traveled from village to village we often stopped at a wayside shop, to buy a soft drink or a snack. Complete strangers would ask us, "Do you have any children? Why don't you have children? Are you taking medicine to prevent having children? Don't you know how to love?"

This was particularly hard on Caroline because she desperately wanted children, and we didn't seem to be able to have them. We lived in hard conditions in the bush, and we often had little to eat and found ourselves ill. Still, Caroline checked her temperature every morning and kept an accurate chart to find the optimal day to conceive. We tried hormone therapy. We even tried a course of contraceptives to see if Caroline could conceive when the course was completed as a rebound. Finally, we had tests done, which showed that we were very unlikely to be able to have children.

For a while we had a study day at Bayanan every Friday, and local preachers came to get help with their Sunday sermons. Also, as Christmas neared, we prepared the Christmas story in drama format straight out of the Gospels, interspersed with traditional Christmas carols, and involved the whole community.

The only baby in the village was a girl, so she was the one taking the place of the baby Jesus, and her parents acted the parts of Mary and Joseph. The prophetess Anna was portrayed by the mother of one of the village leaders, a man named Juan Abat. She prayed so sweetly for the baby. Carding Bulaklak had the role of the angel Gabriel, robed in a sheet off our bed. Every towel and curtain from our house was needed to dress people up, and the choir of angels had wings made of banana leaves.

During this time, we also did a number of projects to set people up in business. We bought a cross-cut saw and lent it to people. They cut down big trees, hollowed them out, and when the river was in flood they floated them down the river to the ocean to sell to fishermen for "bancas" (boats with outriggers).

Caroline went to the market and bought clothes to sell to the local ladies at cost. Lots of women came to our house dressed in a dirty brownish cloth, tied under their armpits. This was how they usually dressed in the mountainous areas.

A couple of teenagers who regularly worked for lowland farmers decided to purchase store-bought clothes from their earnings. After buying bright yellow and orange slips and bras, they paraded up and down the village with their bright new clothes on top of the old mud-colored clothes for everyone to see their new underwear.

We then gave a consignment of clothes and some other goods to two disabled men, Ninardo and Baling, to sell. They were both crippled and impoverished and couldn't go out to the fields like others did. Ninardo was Palai's younger brother, and he had horrible back problems with severe pain. Baling had picked up elephantiasis from parasites in the rice fields which swelled his legs like an elephant's legs. Despite these challenges, they kept their store running for many years.

After four years, as Caroline and I prepared to leave for our second furlough, we taught health classes and trained certain individuals in each village to be "paramedics." We left a box of medicines with them and told them to charge people the cost of these medicines so they could go to town and replenish their supplies. But before we left, we had one last assignment.

One of the New Tribes missionaries who had worked at Tarubong—the former location of their training base—was now the principal of the Philippine Missionary Fellowship Bible School near Manila. I taught a course in John's Gospel there. I had prepared simple pre-tests, and after the day's study there was a post-test. One of the students looked at the test at the end of the first day and said, "You have been teaching John chapter one all day. What can I possibly tell you about this chapter that you don't know?" He had totally misunderstood what a test question is.

We also had a preaching class, which brought a lot of laughter. All the students had to act like someone in a village they might visit in an evangelistic effort. They acted out all the excuses, objections and guff they received when trying to explain the gospel. Then every weekend the students were assigned to visit different villages to preach.

Not long afterwards, at the end of the Bible school at Pambuhan, we held a conference for the surrounding churches. This Bible school had started when one Hanonoo man, who later called himself Jeremiah, asked where he could go to learn about the Scriptures to prepare himself to be a missionary to his own people. The Bible school was originally mobile, set up in multiple areas. Later, it was built in a permanent location, with its own rice fields and a cement path between the buildings.

For the conference, I had a message prepared based on Acts 20, Paul's farewell address to the elders of the church at Ephesus. One after another, the students and other preachers spoke, telling how they had come to the Lord. The conference meetings went on for nine hours that day, so I decided that the message was for me, not for the Mangyan churches.

The testimonies of these men were very similar. They decided to become Christians when the missionary arrived. The missionary told them to *sumampalataya* (believe), but they didn't understand what that was. They kept attending meetings. The missionaries taught them to read. One night by the light of a little kerosene lamp, they read and read, and suddenly the Holy Spirit illuminated the message and they understood. They prayed to receive the Lord.

I had gone to the Philippines expecting to convert the "heathen" through my preaching. I had been brought up on the song:

If you obey the call,
God will be all in all.
Souls at his feet will fall,
Your joy be full.

But it was when these people read the Scriptures for themselves, and the Holy Spirit enlightened them, that they were born again. It wasn't my preaching that brought them to the Lord.

To prepare for leaving the country, Caroline and I had to attend a number of government offices in Manila to get our clearance papers.

While there, we visited some other ministries. From Manila we flew into Hong Kong, where we joined a chartered flight for missionaries which took us to Amman, Jordan, and from there we took a bus to a hotel on the Mount of Olives. This was a very special, though short, "extra" to the cheapest flight home.

We stayed there for two days and had guided tours of Jerusalem. Because all of us were Protestant missionaries, we refused to buy the holy candles on sale outside every church. Without candles it was very difficult to see anything inside these old dark buildings. After visiting the main churches of Jerusalem, and the Church of the Nativity in Bethlehem, we finally visited Gordon's Calvary and the Garden Tomb. It was thrilling to stand at the door to the Garden Tomb, look inside, and remember the angel's words: "He is not here . . . he is risen" (Matthew 28.6 KJV).

On the way back to the airport, we saw Jericho and the Dead Sea. From Amman we flew to Brussels, where we missed our plane to London. We had to spend part of the night in a hotel, and got to London the following day.

From London we went directly to Glasgow where we were met at the railway station by a former missionary and doctor who was going to help us. Dr Murray had been a missionary in China until his son Ian developed polio. He and his family had returned home to the UK 20 years before, and he was now working as a physician in Glasgow. His son Ian was at the Bible Training Institute there. We took Caroline straight to a hospital. Under a general anesthetic all the remaining lumps of penicillin were finally removed!

We bought a used car and traveled about 6,000 miles around the UK. We visited friends, and spoke at missionary meetings and home prayer meetings. We joined Uncle Jimmie and his wife Christine at his Scottish camp. We found the weather hard to adjust to, and people laughed at us. We were wearing every piece of clothing we owned to keep warm in the Scottish summer.

After working in the camps, we went to Keswick, in the English Lake District, for the Keswick Convention. We heard many of the best British preachers, and spent time with missionaries and believers from around the world.

After the Keswick Convention we drove south to Wales and had a weekend with my cousin Ernst in Cardiff. As the Nazis were gaining control of Czechoslovakia, Ernst could only do one thing well: swim. He was a member of an all-Jewish swimming team. Although his team won all the preliminary races, it was prevented from entering the Berlin Olympics of 1936. Ernst worked so hard on his swimming that he was invited to participate in a swimming gala in London.

In 1938 he came to the UK as a member of a swimming team, and after the competition asked for asylum. He served in the Czech army for part of the Second World War, and married the daughter of a Czech who had brought a Bohemian lace machine with him and had set up a lace factory in the UK.

Ernst's father-in-law bought some land just outside Cardiff, built a house on part of the land, and sold the rest of it when the price of the land increased in value. After some years there was a fire and the lace factory was burned down. When the factory was rebuilt, Ernst replaced the hand-operated machines with electric machines, which needed far fewer people. The local population was predictably angry about the loss of jobs. We had an opportunity to see this factory.

We would also have liked to see the synagogue attended by Ernst and his family. But that weekend the rabbi was away so they didn't go to services, and we were not able to visit their synagogue. We showed them our slide pictures and told them about what we were doing, sharing the good news of Christ. Shortly after our visit Ernst sent me a letter saying, "Please don't write to me again." It pained him to see that his younger, Jewish cousin was now a missionary for Christ.

On the way north, we stopped off at Burnley, in Lancashire, to visit a nephew of Miss Corson. He was a doctor in the Royal Air Force and performed surgery on pilots and crewmen injured in the air. Later, he worked as a general practitioner in the area his wife came from. She had been his operating nurse before they fell in love. When Dr Corson retired he moved to Connel, and had a practice in his aunt's house, which he inherited. After our visit, we drove across the north of England to Skipsea where Uncle Jimmie was conducting his English camp.

Then it was back to Scotland. There we met up with OMF friends and spoke at missionary meetings throughout the country. We also visited Miss Corson and gave talks in the Oban area. Yet, as we left, one meaningful moment stood out among the rest.

In Skipsea, Caroline found her way to the Methodist chapel in the village, and poured out her heart to the Lord. A soft smile filled her face as she exited.

"Tom," she told me, "God met me there, and I'm convinced he is going to give us a baby."

God had met our heart's desires by giving us missionary work and good friends around the globe. Now it was time for my faith to join Caroline's, and trust that God would give us a child.

12

Welcoming children
1966–1967

I took Caroline's hand as we sat across the table from a social worker. A friend had driven us to San Francisco to visit an adoption agency. We had been talking and dreaming about a family, and after years of longing this could be our opportunity.

Social worker Millicent Hagerback talked to us for hours, asking us many questions about our life and work. She told us later that she had never had such a long interview before. We were nervous: would she really consider us or would anything come of the application?

"We will consider you," Ms Hagerback finally told us, "but know that this is the first of five interviews. There will also be a visit to your home to see if it is adequate."

Caroline and I exchanged glances. We didn't have a home. We had been vagabonds for many months. We had flown into New York, and my cousin John and his wife Hilda met us at the airport. We visited the OMF representative in New York, and then we had prepaid long-distance bus tickets to travel anywhere in the USA within 99 days for $99. We used these tickets well, attending a missionary conference in Kansas, and family in Flagstaff, Arizona, and in San Diego.

In San Jose, Mom and Pop Bergen—Caroline's second parents—had met us. Both of her birth parents had died from cancer when she was still a young woman. We stayed with the Bergens for some time, and they made a place for us at their cabin at Mount Hermon conference center. Now both Caroline and I knew it was time to find a more permanent place—a place to raise children.

"We have another question." Caroline's gaze met the social worker's. "Is it possible we could have two babies? I know it's a lot to ask, but we are already thirty-six and thirty-seven years old."

Ms Hagerback nodded and jotted down a note. "No promises, of course, but we can see what can be done."

Hope grew in my heart at the thought of having two children. Typically, children of missionaries went to boarding school, and we thought it would be much better for our child to go with a sibling.

Our furlough allowance was about $200 a month, so when we got back to Santa Cruz we looked for rented housing that would possibly be within our price range. There were summer cottages along the waterfront. The lady showing these cottages to us said they would not be adequate in the winter without heating. However, she introduced us to a man preparing a house across the street which he was planning to rent for $120 a month, plus utilities. We talked to him about why we were looking for a house. We learned that he had an adopted daughter, and she in turn also had an adopted daughter. He was very sympathetic. We asked if he could lower the rent to $80, including utilities. He did. This house was sufficient for us. It was close to the beach, to Twin Lakes Baptist Church, and the bus line.

Ten weeks after our first interview, we received a call. "Mr and Mrs Graumann, please come. We have two babies for you."

By this time we had our own car. We drove to San Francisco, and tears of joy filled our eyes as two lovely babies were placed into our arms, fully dressed, from caps to shoes. One boy and one girl. Timothy Andrew Graumann born November 2, 1966, and Lynette Ruth Graumann born November 4, 1966: Tim and Lyn. They were both nearly three months old.

Because of our small missionary allowance, the agency waived the adoption fee of $500 for each to $5 for both. They were willing to waive the fee altogether, but we said, "We can pay that." The agency gave us some items for the babies, and we added those things to the gifts given to us by friends. The number of items overwhelmed us. We weren't sure what babies needed. We were used to village kids in the rainforest, wrapped in their parents' old clothes.

Caroline thought she was getting a cold or even the flu, so she wore a mask when we went to pick up the babies. We arrived home at about 4 p.m. Before going home for dinner, Pastor Kraft, the pastor of Twin Lakes Baptist Church, came to the house and held the babies. It was a

Wednesday, and we took them to the midweek meeting at church. The next morning we took them to the ladies' meeting. They were passed from one to another and thoroughly enjoyed by everyone.

Yet Caroline and I did not adjust well to new parenthood. The babies' needs were overwhelming, and the afternoons were especially hard with their crying. Caroline went to work, and the babies' care was left up to me. I had no experience and found myself frustrated most of the time. We were at the church whenever the doors were open, and I would sink into the pew with a sigh of relief after passing my children to the workers in the church nursery.

It took several weeks for us to get a photo of the babies. We didn't have a camera. During a river crossing in the Philippines, just before coming home, my camera had gotten wet and no longer functioned. Eventually we got a picture and wrote a letter to our OMF leaders, explaining how the Lord had blessed us with these two beautiful babies. We recognized that the Lord had clearly answered our prayer and directed our path. Yet their response was not what we had expected.

We immediately received several letters from OMF leaders telling us that we had disqualified ourselves from missionary service, and we were not welcome to return to the Philippines. Because we had been granted permission to adopt one baby, not two, we were going beyond what we were allowed. This was a great disappointment to us and a bitter pill to swallow. We believed we had met all the conditions the mission leaders had set before we could adopt.

I was in the USA on a British passport with a visitor's visa, and was not allowed to work. The future looked bleak in spite of our joy in having these lovely babies. Twin Lakes Baptist Church was very supportive. We team-taught a Sunday school class and led a department of the Vacation Bible School.

Caroline applied for work as a nurse at a private hospital, and was told that she would need a pre-employment physical. During the check-up the physician, Dr Sundean, asked her, "Do you know you are pregnant?"

This came as a real surprise to us after numerous tests had shown we had no chance of having children. That "flu" she had when we picked up the babies wasn't the flu at all.

While teaching at the Mangyan Bible School (MBS), I became aware of my need for further Bible study so I had enrolled in a correspondence course with London Bible College. I was allowed to do some of my study at Twin Lakes Baptist Church. Now I wanted to take my studies to a higher academic level. One of the Bergens' sons, Ray, had attended seminary and gave us some guidelines for choosing a seminary. We decided to move to Denver, Colorado, so that I could attend Conservative Baptist Seminary.

We sold most of our few possessions and loaded up our old secondhand car with our two babies and all our earthly possessions and drove to Denver. We found the seminary on the edge of Cheesman Park. We walked up and down the streets close by and found a one-bedroom apartment, with a dining room and a living room, which was very suitable for us and which we could rent for $80 a month.

We moved in soon after. There was a window looking out onto the road, and the children spent hours gazing out of the window at whatever was passing along the street, and the construction on the other side.

Caroline applied for a job at the nearest hospital and completed her orientation. On the first night she worked, our baby's head dropped and she had difficulty walking, so she had to stop work.

I studied at the seminary as a special student because I didn't have a bachelor's degree. I didn't expect to be able to keep up with the graduate students, but I wanted to learn what I could. I took a lot of missions courses. The evening before a missions test, Caroline's waters broke. At that time we were attending a Baptist church in Littleton, Colorado, and were on close terms with the pastor. So, as arranged, I took Tim and Lyn to the home of Pastor Knight, so he and his wife could take care of them.

Caroline and I then waited till after midnight, because we knew that the hospital charge for the day began at midnight. At that point I walked a block down the street to a public phone and called the doctor and the hospital. I took Caroline to the hospital, and she was immediately admitted to the labor department.

Daniel (Dan) John Graumann was born at 6 a.m. on October 27, 1967. When the nurse brought him to us, he had not been cleaned up and was very blue. Not knowing anything about babies, I thought this was normal for newborns. That day I went to seminary, after a sleepless night, took my test, and returned to the hospital.

One of the families in the church paid for the first month of diaper service. This service covered laundering all the diapers, and the children's clothes too if we wanted them cleaned, at the same price. The first week the driver, who was profoundly deaf and unable to speak, arrived and was surprised at the big bag of diapers we gave him. He pushed down on the bag and found it was actually full. We showed him the three babies, so he understood. We continued this service till we left Denver, one and a half years later.

My mind and heart were still set on missionary service. Through the seminary I got a scholarship to attend a students' missionary conference at Urbana, Illinois. Then, after one and a half years at seminary, I applied to the Conservative Baptist Foreign Missionary Society (CBFMS), and we flew to Chicago with Dan. We had left Tim and Lynette with Pastor Knight and his wife. Don and Anna Ford came to the CBFMS headquarters at Wheaton, Illinois, picked Dan up, and took care of him while we attended the orientation school. Anna had been Caroline's roommate for one year at Prairie Bible Institute in Alberta, Canada. Most of that week, Caroline felt very nauseated, and we discovered she was pregnant again. Even with our growing family, we were accepted and appointed as missionary candidates.

During the week we were in Wheaton, we visited Rochunga Pudaite and his wife, who headed up the ministry of Bibles for the World, with headquarters in Wheaton. Rochunga, my fellow student at BTI, Glasgow, told us how the USSR had an education material exchange program with India, and Rochunga saw this as an opportunity to send Bibles from India to Russia, using the telephone directory for addresses. This was so successful that he got more telephone directories for other countries. This ministry grew to become "Bibles for the World."

We flew back to Denver and prepared to leave Denver for Santa Cruz where we had become missionary candidates raising support. In addition to participating in missionary conferences and summer camps, I worked part-time as an orderly at Santa Cruz General Hospital. The administrators didn't like to have a qualified nurse working as an orderly, but without a license as a California registered nurse (RN) I couldn't work as a nurse. After that, I obtained a work visa, and later became a US citizen through marriage.

Even though I traveled often for missionary service, I was home for the birth of our next baby, Paul. I remember as we were wheeling Caroline into the delivery room that a woman came out screaming about losing her baby. This was unnerving, especially as Dr Sundean had to deliver Paul carefully. The cord was wrapped three times around his neck. Dr Sundean cut the cord, and Paul was delivered very quickly.

After the tests—for both of us—had proved that we couldn't have a baby, we now had four precious children. Mom Bergen invited us to the Mount Hermon cabin, and she took care of Caroline and the children after Paul was born. I spent my time attending spring missionary conferences in northern California and Oregon.

On one visit home, the whole family was down with the flu. I flew back to Portland, rented a little car, and went to the church where I was to speak that evening. I felt hot. My throat was sore. I needed to stand close to the microphone to make myself heard. I continued with my schedule of meetings, but I had to hold on to the pulpit so I didn't fall over backward.

I arrived at one church on my itinerary and found the meeting had been canceled, so I went to the pastor who organized the meetings in that area. He invited me to stay at his home and took me with him on some visits. As he started his car, I had a pain at the back of my head. I had difficulty turning my head, so it was scary driving on the highways. When I had completed the scheduled meeting, I drove back to the CBFMS office in Portland, Oregon. When I arrived, Dave Billing—a CBFMS missionary friend I had met in Manila—was unloading a shipment of books. I asked him to call Caroline and tell her I was coming home.

Caroline and I had minimal health insurance under CBFMS, so the doctor told us we had to register with welfare (the US benefit system) before he could examine me. By this time, I couldn't walk without assistance. I was admitted to Dominican Hospital in Santa Cruz for a week of tests.

Soon I lost the use of my hands, and it became impossible even to mark my diet sheet for what I wanted to eat. The nurses gave me a bed bath, as I lay there completely helpless.

Pastor Kraft came to visit and pray for me. As he prayed, I felt sure I was going to recover from this illness, but the test results were shocking. I was diagnosed with cerebellar ataxia—a disorder that occurs when the cerebellum becomes inflamed and damaged. I had lost all coordination and had difficulty performing daily tasks. I couldn't coordinate my torso, arms or legs. I couldn't walk, and had slurred speech and trouble eating. Headaches plagued me daily, but with no more they could do for me, the doctors decided to send me home.

Giving me little hope of recovery, the discharging doctor wanted to register me as permanently disabled.

"No, I am sorry. I will not accept that," I told him. I thought of Pastor Kraft's prayer and the peace I had felt. "I will recover," I added with determination.

While we were on welfare, we were getting much more cash and food supplies than we were used to. At the end of the year, we decided to get off welfare and repeatedly returned welfare checks until the authorities finally stopped sending them to us. With hindsight, we should have stayed on longer because it took me three years to recover enough to function.

Caroline worked the evening shifts at the Adventist hospital four days a week. A young neighbor came regularly to play with the children and did a lot of babysitting for us, at 50 cents an hour, for the four. She came after school and stayed till she put the children to bed. She was very good until she became interested in boys and then things weren't so good. Caroline would come home and find the children in bed without any sheets or blankets, just lying on the plastic sheet. If Paul woke up before Caroline came home from work, I was able to pick him up and rock him, but my movements were so jerky that I usually woke him up again trying to put him back in his crib.

I was just recovering enough to get around, although I couldn't walk in a straight line or without jerks, when there was a Conservative Baptist conference in San Jose. I went there for several meetings. I was looking forward to this very much, but when I got there I encountered a problem. On arrival, everyone stood around in the area between the food counter and the tables. After prayer, we were invited to come to the counter, pick up a tray of food, and carry it to one of the tables and eat. I knew that was impossible for me, and in frustration and embarrassment I broke down in tears, knowing there was no way I could carry the tray to a table. Miserably I stood to the side, out of the way. Finally, someone who recognized me offered to carry a tray to a table for me.

Caroline was working part-time at the Adventist hospital as well as caring for the family. Her workload was immense, and unsurprisingly she developed severe back pain. She applied for unemployment benefit but didn't receive it. She gritted her teeth and carried on, and eventually there was some improvement.

As my health began to improve I started attending classes at Cabrillo Junior College near Santa Cruz, California. Several times I got calls from the registration office: "Please come and sign your application papers." I still had limited control over my movements, so kept putting it off, hoping to be able to write soon. Thankfully, before the end of the first quarter, I was able to write and take my exams. It was a tough time: we didn't get any missionary support or training after my health failed. We felt discouraged, yet the mission field was still the goal.

I prayed from my heart: "Lord, will this ever be possible?"

13

Home
1970–1976

The sound of children's voices filled the air, and I smiled to myself as Caroline and I worked together in the garage. This wasn't the life I had expected to live. We had planned to live and serve overseas. Sometimes I questioned why our heart's desire was denied, yet Caroline and I both trusted God. We would work to our best ability where we were, knowing there were people in our town who needed to hear the gospel too.

I had mostly recovered, despite the doctor's dire predictions, and Caroline and I worked opposite nursing shifts. Our house had a huge yard (what the British call a garden) with fruit trees and raspberry plants—and, unfortunately, gophers. We planted tomatoes, and Caroline always had the children involved in helping her with projects.

One afternoon, as we sewed scraps of carpet together to cover the back-bedroom floor, we heard a noise above our heads. We looked up. A saw blade slashed through the ceiling. Dan wanted to install a "fireman's pole" to be able to get quickly out of the attic, but we halted his efforts. Evidently, he had thought if he cut the round hole, the pole would follow.

Tim and Lyn started school, and we became involved as school volunteers. I also served in a local coffee house, run by two men at our church. This was at the height of the hippie movement. One customer looked just like the typical image of Jesus in popular picture books. He called himself "Jesus," and he said he was waiting for the right time to walk on the water across Monterey Bay.

I studied more, working through a number of nursing textbooks, and after several failures, eventually passed the California RN exam and got my nursing license. I took a night supervisor's job at an extended care facility for people with serious or terminal conditions, but it was hard dealing with so many deaths. The experience created an even greater urge in me to share the gospel and prepare people for eternity, but I never felt I did as much as I should have done.

In preparation for the Billy Graham crusade at Oakland, California, in 1971, there were series of counselor training classes. As the crusade started, I drove to Oakland every evening to counsel and pray with those who had made decisions for Christ, just as I had done in Glasgow and Manila.

Soon, I got my associate of arts degree in liberal arts at Cabrillo College and also enrolled in Bethany Bible College. The administrators asked me to list all the classes I had taken. I included my seminary classes in the list. The admissions department gave me all of these as credit toward my bachelor of science degree (BS). This cut off one and a half years of seminary study from my load.

After I graduated from Bethany, we prepared to move back to Denver. I went for an interview at Craig Hospital, a rehabilitation hospital for people with spinal cord injuries, and got an evening shift RN position.

As we again searched for a house, four-year-old Paul had a final word before we set out one day: "Look for a house with a tree and lots of flowers."

Late in the afternoon we came to a house on University Boulevard, Denver, which had a semicircular driveway, a few trees, lots of dandelions and a big yard. We loved the place and took it. Our church provided furniture.

Once the family was moved over, I enrolled in the seminary and left early in the morning for classes. Then I went straight to Craig Hospital, worked the evening shift, and got home late.

Dan was now aged seven and in second grade at school. One day, his teacher was discussing roles in the family and asked Dan to tell the class a little about his father.

"My daddy goes to school, and cooks," he said. "My daddy is also a drug pusher," he added, because he had seen me with a medication cart at work, and I had often joked about prompting patients to take their meds.

"Oh no," the teacher gasped. "I met your dad at the teacher–parent conference, and he is a nice man."

Yet, even as busy as life was, Caroline and I still had a passion for missions. Even when we ourselves were not serving in that way, we gave as much as we could to other missionaries, knowing their needs from our own experience. I was also able to join a mission trip to Mexico in 1976. We traveled around that country, and with great joy I saw the gospel being preached to the poor.

Caroline and I also opened our home to seminary students, allowing them to live with us. Among these was a young man named Karl Helwig, son of a doctor. Karl played with the kids, including hide-and-seek in the dark, and he taught them the Greek alphabet. He was more a part of our family than probably any of the other seminary students who lived with us. Karl also read Tolkien's *The Hobbit* and C. S. Lewis's Narnia series to the kids.

As the children were growing up, there were always things around the house that needed to be done. We installed sprinkler systems, and the kids picked up and washed pebbles and replaced them around the outside of the house. We laid cement paths and planted trees. The children learned to persevere, even if they didn't like the jobs.

Among our patients on the evening shift at Craig hospital were several believers, but some of them seemed to find it even harder than unbelievers to accept their injuries, hoping for healing instead of getting down to the hard work of rehabilitation. Often I lent them a listening ear. They knew I understood, having gone through something similar myself.

While holding down a full-time job, I worked many extra shifts for temporary services, providing cover for staff or short-term vacancies. Caroline also did this, working mostly for CPQ Nurses. These agencies sent us to hospitals and nursing homes all over the city and beyond.

During the time I worked at Craig, I did many double shifts. There were orderlies at the hospital whose job involved turning patients according to a set schedule to prevent their skin from breaking down. But often, when I needed to change a dressing, I was accustomed to turning patients without help, and I must have burst a lumbar disc doing this. I had a lot of back pain, to the point where I went from patient to patient in a wheel-chair for the last few days before undergoing back surgery.

To allow Caroline to stay home and still earn some money, we became a receiving home for children in foster care through a program run by the local government of Arapahoe County. We were licensed to take in eight children under 12 years of age. The first children were four sisters who had been abused by their mother and were starving for love.

A social worker brought two little African American children to our home one evening. Caroline put them into a warm bath. The little girl, about five years old, had a mark on her skin in the shape of an iron.

"What's this?" Caroline asked.

"My momma don't like me," she replied.

We had children of all ages, and every evening after dinner we read the Bible, sang songs, and prayed with the kids. Mission Hills Church was very supportive when we took them to church with us.

We tried to keep the children busy with activities rather than sitting around watching TV. One evening two of the boys were arguing at the table. Caroline warned them to stop, but they continued arguing. At this, she gave them one swat on the leg with a wooden spoon.

One boy immediately called his parents: "Mrs Graumann is beating us."

Within 24 hours all eight of the foster kids were taken away and placed in other homes. This ban stayed in effect, and looking back, I feel it was probably good for our own children, who needed more attention.

At the time, we lived on a busy road, and after numerous traffic accidents nearby we decided we had to move. The final straw came when, to our horror, Dan was hit by a car: he was dragged along the street for a few yards, but miraculously was unharmed. We also lost a few pets. After a search, we found a house that suited us but needed a lot of work. This didn't worry us too much as we had become quite adept at making repairs. (In addition to fixing up our own houses, Caroline also started fixing up rented properties. Our children helped in all aspects and became hard workers.)

When Lynette turned 14, she signed up to work part-time at Cherrylyn Manor, a private nursing home, with me. Fourteen-year-olds could only be "candy-stripers"—hospital volunteers who usually wore red-and-white striped pinafores—carrying out basic tasks, such as delivering flowers, or giving ice water to patients. Lynette wanted to do what the other aides were doing, and for the most part, she did.

Our Sterne Parkway house was about a half-mile from Arapahoe Community College where Spring International had a school to teach

English to international students. One of their services was to find host families for students. Families were encouraged to take on students who spoke different languages, but not more than one person for each language so that everyone was forced to communicate in English. Through the years, we had students from many different countries living with us: South American nations, various Arab countries, Japan, Thailand and Taiwan.

One student, Peter Tami from Thailand, called us and said he couldn't understand what his college professors were trying to teach him. He asked if he could live with us and study at Spring International Language School. Peter became like a son to us. We worked with him on his homework, especially with his final-term paper about the effect of the gospel on his culture.

Peter celebrated his birthday at our house with a big party. He invited everyone at Spring International. Some brought food they had cooked at home, while others cooked when they came to our place.

When Dan came home he looked around. "Mom! It's wall-to-wall people and no one speaks English."

He was entirely wrong, in one sense: in fact, all these people—from Bolivia, Sri Lanka, Oman, Saudi Arabia, Iran, Iraq, Thailand, Korea, Japan and so on—could only communicate through using English.

At our international parties we often displayed people's national flags. One of the Arab students, Muhammad, said to me, "I don't like to see the flag of Israel beside the flag of my country."

"That's very interesting," I replied. "You don't mind eating in the home of a Jew, but you don't like the flag of his country."

One evening we took this young man to see a Christian magician perform tricks as a means of explaining the gospel. Muhammad insisted, "If I knew that God was alive, I would believe in him."

He frequently complained of headaches and would go to the Emergency Room of the local hospital, which was a very expensive way to get an aspirin.

"Next time you have a headache, come and get Tom or me," Caroline told him. "We're both nurses, and we'll give you something for it."

The next headache happened while I was at work and Caroline was at Mission Hills Church, practicing for the Easter Cantata. Muhammad went to the church, heard a very impressive presentation on the resurrection, and got his headache pill. Over the course of the Easter weekend he heard the Cantata three times.

"Now I believe God is alive," he said at the end of the week.

We gave him a Bible. He came to church with us and appeared to be a believer. Yet when his uncle came over from Egypt to straighten out his finances, Muhammad gave the Bible back to us. After he returned to Egypt with his uncle he wrote to say, "I'm no longer a Christian." We were saddened to hear this, yet we hoped that the root of the gospel planted in his heart would grow nevertheless.

While our children were still at home, we listened to a Bible story or read from the Bible every evening after dinner. We told our students it was good practice in English. Before the Billy Graham Denver crusade, we attended the counselor training classes. Peter Tami was a believer, and these were good classes for him. He invited the other students, including Muslims, to come with us, and to our delight one of our Arab students completed an application to become a counselor.

When Peter went to Bible college in the Los Angeles area, he sent another student, Mika, from Japan, to our home. She was a seeker, and very open. We read the Bible together every evening, and she would come to church with us. We introduced her to the Japanese church in Denver, where finally she was challenged by someone who asked, "What are you waiting for? Why don't you accept Jesus as Savior?"

Mika was timid. She had read a book about the persecution of one of the first Japanese to believe in Jesus. Yet finally the truth won out, and it was a joy to witness her baptism at the Japanese Christian Church.

Tim and Lynette attended Heritage High School and participated in the marching band. Lynette made many friends, took a lot of her academic courses early, and during her last semester was able to follow mostly "fun" courses, such as swimming, life-saving, sewing, and cooking. She left school with a swimming instructor's certificate and a life-saving certificate and got a job at the YMCA pool.

Tim, by contrast, pretended to go to school long after he had actually dropped out. He intercepted the mail so we didn't get the letters from the school about him.

When Lynette was in high school she became interested in horses.

Caroline called me one evening while I was working, telling me about a horse she had found advertised for sale.

"Can we buy a horse?"

"We can't afford a horse," I responded.

"By the time we can afford a horse, Lynette will be gone," was her reply.

So we bought a horse, Dee. Her owner had bred her, and we found a stable near the school where she could be boarded for $50 a month. In due course Dee gave birth to a foal, Brandy Saxet, in the middle of a storm, but the little creature died soon after birth. Dee was bred again and the foal became Lynette's. She called it Crystal. Every day after school Lynette took care of Crystal and went riding on Dee. After Lynette got married she sold Crystal and donated Dee to Camp Id-Ra-Ha-Je, which stood for "I'd Rather Have Jesus."

Because of Lynette's love for horses, Tim also developed an interest, and eventually got a job with a European riding stable, taking care of horses between shows. He traveled from state to state for some time, taking care of the horses, which participated in riding competitions. I thought that traveling from state to state at his employer's expense was a wonderful educational experience!

When Lynette graduated from Heritage High School, she spent her first summer working as a wrangler at Camp Id-Ra-Ha-Je. She saddled horses, took care of them, and took campers for horse-rides along the trails.

A young man, Alan Rice, who had come to the Lord at Englewood Christian Church, a popular fellowship in a neighboring district, was leader of Tepee Camp, which was also a part of Camp Id-Ra-Ha-Je. He was impressed by Lynette and started to date her. He joined the US Marines and was assigned to a Denver unit initially. After high school, Lynette decided to study at Biola University in southern California. The whole family took her there, and we visited friends and relatives in the area.

Dan found academic study hard. All the way through school, he was in special education. He was much more interested in woodworking. Even while in kindergarten, aged only five, Dan had made a table and stool, and carried it to school to describe it to his classmates during "show-and-tell."

On days when there was a trash collection, people would put out odd materials at the side of the road, and Caroline would pick up items for Dan. He built numerous playhouses between the bushes in the backyard. In due course, however, we got a letter from the City of Littleton ordering us to "remove these unsightly structures." Dan then decided to burrow, and built himself a playhouse underground where no one could see what he had made.

When Dan grew older, one of my nursing assistants said her husband was a framer, who constructed the timber skeleton for houses. He needed help pounding nails on the construction site. I called home, and Dan immediately signed up. He worked after school and on Saturdays. During his senior year, he took up furniture-making, saying he couldn't do framing for the rest of his life. He won a medal for a roll-top desk set he made and presented at a state-wide competition. On graduation he got several job offers from cabinet-makers.

In junior high school, Paul was small, and he had a lot of problems with the bigger kids teasing him. He also wanted to work with Dan on the construction site. So we decided he could study through Liberty Academy as a homeschooler and have a job part-time. We sent for a supply of books, and I sat down with Paul to discuss what he was going to do and left him to work on his own.

At the beginning, Paul studied all morning and went to work in the afternoon. Later he worked one day and studied the next. More than once, when he was on the job site, he was sent home because he was too young, yet he was a hard worker. He completed 18 months of study in one year, and took a General Educational Development (GED) test.

One day, the boys took the cracked floor-tiles off the basement playroom floor because we were having flooding in the basement. The floor was covered with black tile adhesive. The next morning I was off work, so while Paul was studying in his room, I started washing the adhesive off with gasoline. It was coming off very well. I was working on my hands and knees, with a gasoline-soaked cloth in both hands. Suddenly the gas caught on fire, and the whole basement burst into flames. My hands and pants were on fire. I called to Paul, who fortunately had the door to his room open. He saw me, the air, and the floor all burst into flames, and as the oxygen was pulled out of Paul's room it sucked the door closed. Paul called 911 and related the events and address. He used a towel to open the door of his room to escape. I ran to the freezer to get frozen peas for my hands, and we waited on the front porch.

The agonizing minutes seemed like hours. Running back in, I called the fire department, and we again waited outside. Eventually, help came. The paramedics took us both to Swedish Hospital Emergency Room, where we were checked for smoke inhalation. The fire department put out the fire and boarded up the windows. A hand surgeon worked on my hands, and I came home with both hands wrapped in bandages, and supplies to change the dressings.

The whole house was black with soot and smelled of smoke. We were given an apartment in a housing development, and lived there while the house was being repaired, cleaned and painted. The house was repaired with insurance money, but Caroline soon made it a project for our kids also. They worked on all parts of the construction, helping as they were able. We celebrated Christmas in the apartment. Alan joined us, and on Christmas Eve Alan and Lynette announced their engagement.

Lynette got hold of a book about weddings and studied exactly what should be done and when each event should take place. Caroline planted roses in preparation, and learned how to use wires to hold up the heads of the cut roses to prevent them drooping.

After six months, we were back in our Sterne Parkway house, and Alan and Lynette were married at Mission Hills Church. Caroline had some unique ideas about what to serve for refreshments. She wanted to have a potato bar, and Lyn was opposed to that, but Mom wasn't going to be swayed. Overall it worked out fine, and as always happens, families show their quirks during these times.

The day after the wedding, we all went to Alan's parents' house and found the wedding gifts neatly laid out. Amid the general excitement the young couple opened their gifts and left for their honeymoon.

Lynette continued her studies to become a veterinary technician, working with all types of animals. After a while, Alan and Lynette got base housing close to the military hospital, and little Jessica soon joined their family.

While Alan and Lynette were in Aurora in base housing, my cousin Lisl and her husband George visited us from Australia. When George and Lisl got back to Australia they invited us to visit them, and offered to pay half our fare. Looking at the map, we realized that the Philippines lie between the USA and Australia, so we got a visa to visit the Philippines for two months and a visa to go to Australia for a month. We packed, excited with this new adventure and wondering what mission awaited us next.

14

A visit to the Philippines and Australia

1990

The steamy tropical climate of the Philippines welcomed us, yet as we took a taxi from Manila airport to the OMF mission home in Quezon City we recognized little along the way. Everywhere we saw armed guards. New buildings and roads and overhead rail systems had been added, as well as new technology and advertising.

Arriving at the guesthouse, we were greeted with the news that Communist insurgents were active in Mindoro and it would not be safe to go there. Instead we visited Merv and Liz Simons, from New Zealand, working with Gospel Literature Outreach (GLO). They shared their vision to establish English-speaking independent assemblies, which could support church planters. On Sunday morning we attended their service, which was in a horse-riding stable. The building had a roof but no walls, which allowed the breeze to air-condition the building.

Throughout the area, numerous organizations were leading and training Bible students and workers. The Philippine Missionary Institute had a "livelihood project," through which they gave fishing boats or chickens to families so they could support themselves. All the teachers at the school were now Filipinos, but they were teaching in English, and their library was filled with English books. We were sorry to hear of the change from using Tagalog, but happy to see the ongoing education.

We took a flight to Legazpi City and stayed in a hotel, the cheapest and worst we have ever been in. We checked in and went to the local open-air market. There we met some children, and Caroline taught them the "Egg Story" and various children's songs. For the egg story she carried plastic eggs with Christian symbols in them. As they were opened, Caroline was able to tell the gospel story. In the morning we got a bus to Iriga, where two of our former students took us to their home. Caroline went through the egg story with them, and in the morning Rhoda, one of our old students, told this story to some of the local children.

When we returned to Manila, we were given the green light to visit Mindoro. We took a bus to Batangas and found the road much better than we remembered from 25 years earlier. When we got to Batangas pier, we saw a huge tank-landing craft, instead of the little inter-island boats we knew from our early days. The ship was being loaded with jeeps filled to five feet above the roof with produce to sell in the market. Everywhere we saw soldiers and guards with rifles. We had a very pleasant two-hour sail to Calapan, then took a tricycle to Bonbon Hill where the OMF guesthouse is located. We got a warm welcome and met several of the missionaries.

Myrna Dong-On, from the Ifugao area in north Luzon Island, had signed up to be "house mother" to the Mangyan children who were attending school in Calapan. She accompanied us to Bayanan, so she could meet the families of some of the children she would be taking care of. We were amazed at the house built for the missionaries. It had electricity, running water, a flush toilet and a refrigerator.

We had dinner one evening with Bado, the head teacher of the Mangyan Bible School, and his wife Marta.

"We don't need missionaries to teach at this school anymore," he told us. "We can do that. But we still need missionaries to give us advice and help us prepare literature."

I took Caroline's hand in my own as joy filled my heart. The work we had helped to start had made a difference. *We* had made a difference. Twenty-five years before, our mission leaders had told us that these illiterate people from the rainforest couldn't understand Scripture. But they had been wrong.

A few minutes' walk further up the hill, we came to the Far East Broadcasting Company radio station, DZB2, built by Tom and Vicki Tweddell. When they erected the antenna in a good location for broadcasting, they found several young believers within a stone's throw whom they trained to be announcers and interviewers and run the station. This was a unique radio station, without doors or windows. During programs you could hear cocks crowing and dogs barking, but this background noise was very natural. Tom and Vicki had a wide assortment of music on tape, because Tom had already built similar radio stations in Taiwan and Indonesia before coming to the Philippines.

On Sunday morning, long before daylight, people were awake cooking large pots of rice and meat. We gathered at the side of the river, and several people were baptized, and then we went back to the chapel for a time of worship and celebrated the Lord's Supper. At noon we had a big meal with everyone eating together. During the afternoon many people left, but in the evening we had a time of singing, when representatives from different people-groups sang in their own language. This was very enjoyable and went on for hours into the night.

Back in Calapan, we visited Barbara and Russell Reed, who were polishing up their translation of the New Testament in the Tawbuhid language. Russell had developed Parkinson's disease, and as soon as they had their translation ready for printing, they were going to retire.

I remembered from years before how Russell and Barbara had been accepted by the Tawbuhid. Their ancestors had told them that someday some white people, who spoke their language, would come with a book. The people had received the young American couple very warmly. Hundreds turned to the Lord, were baptized, and local churches were established in village after village. They had once been the most primitive group on the island—and the only one that practiced poisoning people—and were now a well-dressed, literate community.

Even as we prepared to leave, Caroline and I wondered if we would come back and work with those who were doing such amazing things among the people of our heart. But before we could think of that, we traveled to Australia. As the plane landed in Melbourne I realized that if timing had been different, and Lisl had found me in Scotland all those years before, I could have called this place my home.

***

George and Lisl Singer met us at the airport and took us to their beautiful apartment on the sixth floor of a high-rise retirement complex. From the window we could see the park below, where cricket teams played every Saturday and Sunday. We enjoyed the swimming pool in the basement, and we hit a tennis ball back and forth, although we didn't really know how to play tennis.

Lisl and George were going to Adelaide with their children for a week of skiing, so they arranged a trip for us. We got onto an almost empty double-decker bus to Canberra, the capital. After coming from the crowded city of Manila, we were struck by the wide-open spaces in Australia, with only a few animals and even fewer people.

We visited friends and worshipped with a church community. From Canberra, we took a bus to Sydney and then a taxi to the home of Lisl's mother, Aunt Camila. Her house was filled with all sorts of mementos and pictures from the past. She insisted on cooking us what she proudly called "*Vienna* schnitzel," showed us photos, and told us stories about how her family had immigrated to Australia not long before I was put on a train to the UK.

Aunt Camila explained the difficult years when none of her family understood English. She narrated the story about their early efforts to find work and the later success of their daughter Lisl, her husband George, and their children, Greg and Mary. Aunt Camila took us for a trip by bus and boat to the other side of Sydney Harbour, to a popular picnic spot.

One day we went downtown on our own and saw the famous Sydney Opera House and the Sydney Harbour Bridge. We then took the bus back to Melbourne, where George and Lisl welcomed us back, and we had a very nice vacation with them, exploring new things. We went to the Holocaust Museum, which Lisl had been involved in setting up. I was amazed at the number of photographs of every detail of life in the concentration camps. Lisl explained that the Nazis were very proud of what they were doing so they took lots of photos.

One Friday evening, we experienced a traditional Sabbath candle-lighting ceremony, complete with prayers in Hebrew. We had Sabbath bread and wine. The next morning Lisl took us to their Reform temple where she was involved in a ladies' ministry. They accompanied us to the Great Synagogue in Melbourne and explained that traditionally there was a curtain between the men's and women's sections so the two groups couldn't see each other.

For our last weekend in Melbourne, we looked up a phone number for "Christian assemblies" in the phone book. We called and were given directions to one assembly that would welcome us.

Yet even as we traveled, I felt a stirring. As we visited each ministry I wondered, "Is this my place, Lord?" Yet soon I would find out that God did have a place for Caroline and me, and it would involve me returning to my first home.

15

A letter from Cousin Honza
1990–1993

My hands trembled as I held in them two letters. We had only been home a short time, and I was now working at Hallmark Nursing Care, a private facility for the elderly. One letter came from my cousin Honza Horský, son of my uncle Beda, and another from Aunt Maria in Prague.

The Communist regime had fallen in Czechoslovakia, and Grandmother's house had been returned to the family. My relatives wanted to sell the house in Brno and needed to know if I would agree. A rush of emotions filled me. I remembered playing in the garden and running down the halls of Grandmother's house. Now it was partly mine after all this time? What condition was it in? How would it feel to stand on the sidewalk and peer up at it once more?

Shortly after making our first contact with my cousin Honza in Prague, I saw an ad for a cheap flight to Frankfurt. Caroline and I booked this flight and called Aunt Maria. She said we needed to arrange a hotel, but we insisted we were going to visit them, not a hotel.

We flew to Frankfurt and caught a train for Prague, which involved a change at the next station. We missed our train connection and were now several hours late. Because we were late, when we got to the German–Czech border we had to get out of the train and take a bus to the other side.

We called Honza to say we were running late.

"Where are you?" he said.

We looked at the sign on the station wall. "Prijezd," I told him. I learned later that meant "Arrivals." (I had completely forgotten the language of my childhood.)

"Is there anyone there who speaks Czech?" Honza asked.

We gave the phone to someone nearby. He spoke to my cousin and helped us out, and then we ran and got on the train.

We sat in a compartment where there was a young soldier. He didn't know any English, but we had a Czech–English phrase book. We found a question, pointed to it, and gave him the book. He found an answer and pointed to it.

With that simple means of communication, we struck up a conversation. The soldier was a border guard whose job was to patrol the border with a dog. He was on his way home to Opava on leave. We gave him a Czech New Testament paraphrase, published by Living Bibles International. We asked him to read aloud, and he read about the first five chapters of Matthew's Gospel.

At Plzen, a group of Danish high-school students got on the train. They were on a sightseeing trip with their teacher. One girl, about 15 years old, came into our compartment. She spoke remarkably good English, so we talked for some time.

In Prague, Honza and his wife Stana were on the platform waiting for us. We asked if it had been difficult to identify us.

"Oh no," he replied. "You were clearly the only Americans on the train."

They took us to Aunt Maria's apartment for the night, and she went to stay at a friend's home. She was back early the next morning, and brought us day passes for the metro and took us sightseeing.

The next day, Stana took us to Prague Castle, and several museums and art galleries. By noon we were tired and would have liked to sit down. At the foot of the castle there were several restaurants, but they were all crowded. The only places available were some high tables at which you could stand and eat. In the evening we met Teresa, their youngest child; Michella, their middle daughter; and Katka their oldest daughter and her boyfriend Tony. We had a very nice Czech dinner.

The next day, Honza and Stana took us to Brno by car. Along the way we saw many small gardens, each with a little house. They explained that most families lived in high-rise apartments, but they also had a garden plot where they could grow flowers, fruit and vegetables. They pointed out the village where Uncle Beda used to live and manage an estate.

In Brno, we went to the real estate office involved with the sale of Grandmother's house. Two people from this office came with us to show us what was left of her home. The house seemed bigger than I remembered, but the large garden was gone and in its place there was a high-rise apartment building. The gardener's house behind ours was also gone. Rain was pouring in where a wall had been removed. There were pools of water on some of the floors. Many windows were missing. All the electric wiring and water pipes and plumbing were gone, including toilets and bathtubs. Back home, Caroline had remodeled many wood-frame houses, but this would have been a much bigger project than she could have tackled.

We agreed to sell Grandmother's house and split the proceeds. On completion of the sale, my portion was put into a Czech bank account for me, with the government stipulation that it could only be spent inside the country, which opened up creative thinking for new opportunities. These funds gave us a security cushion for 22 years of ministry there, and money to help others, some of which is still supporting Christian work in the region.

We stopped at a little restaurant along the way, ate lunch, and then drove into Těšany.

The old *zamek* where I had lived from ages five to eight was deserted. The rooms were bare and filthy. The large cowshed, which used to have about 80 dairy cows, was also empty. There was no one there and nothing around the estate.

We went round to the back where the garden used to be. One wall remained, with a big hole. Through this hole we could see an area of waist-high weeds, but no neat paths, flowerbeds, vegetable plants or fruit trees. Memories of time spent here with my mother and Tony overwhelmed me. All I had known was now in shambles, just as all those I had known were gone.

It was a quiet drive back to Prague, as all of us were lost in our own thoughts.

The next day, Honza and Stana took us to the railway station and put us on a train for Budapest. At the Hungarian border crossing, police officers examined our passports. A man named Andreas and his mother Magda met us at the station in Budapest. They were relatives descended from Grandfather's sister. We went to Andreas's apartment and were introduced to his old mother-in-law, who lived with them. Andreas's wife had died in a car accident several years earlier. Two of his sons spoke to us in English. They were ready to take us to a hotel, but we saw there was an empty room in their apartment, so we slept there.

In the morning, Andreas took us to see the castle. He explained that the city had a street plan showing where all the houses had been before the Second World War, and in most cases the buildings destroyed in the war had now been replaced where they had stood. He took us to the bank to exchange our traveler's checks for Hungarian forints. Then we went to the bus station to buy tickets to Vienna. The official there refused to take Hungarian currency for tickets for someone traveling with a US passport. So we had a lot of Hungarian money.

At a metro station, we saw Mormon missionaries selling books. We asked them for the location of a Christian bookstore. There, we bought numerous books for our relatives, including one about J. Hudson Taylor. We explained to them that he was the founder of the missionary organization with which we worked in the Philippines. We were invited to Magda's apartment for special Hungarian ham sandwiches.

From Budapest we went to Vienna in a double-decker bus. We were in the front seat upstairs, and had a beautiful view of the countryside. When the Austrian police came to check people's passports at the border, they examined some closely, but hardly looked at the US passports.

Nikki Hereford was waiting for us at the bus station. Nikki was a distant relative closer to the family of Magda. She was born in Kenya, spoke fluent English, and worked as a volunteer for the Anglican Church in Vienna. She had some appointments that evening which she could not miss so she took us to a train station. There we met a lady who had a pension for rent and was looking for customers. Her place was close to the station. She showed us a room with a number of beds and a kitchen where we could prepare our own food. We went to a shop, found something to eat, and brought it home.

We called Martha Heidinger of Child Evangelism Fellowship (CEF) and arranged to meet her at the YMCA where the International Church had a Sunday service. When we got to this service, we noticed a lot of Filipinos. Visitors were invited to introduce themselves, so we greeted everyone in Tagalog. While waiting for Martha, we talked to a number of the Filipinos who were changing their babies' diapers after the service.

Martha told us about her visits to Czechoslovakia, her contacts there and her plans to set up a national CEF office. We encouraged her to move to Czechoslovakia, stay there, and learn the language. She drove us around Vienna, showed us St Stephen's Cathedral, invited us to her apartment for a cup of tea, and then took us back to our room. The next day was a holiday, and all the museums and art galleries were admission free. We spent the whole day going from one to another.

We arranged to meet Nikki at a restaurant behind the Opera House. We only saw one restaurant—in front of the Opera House—and waited there. She waited for us behind the Opera House, so we didn't meet up, and we were all very upset about standing in the cold and missing each other. Caroline and I then took an overnight train to Frankfurt, which saved paying for a night's lodging, and from there we flew home. We had found this trip to be a very eye-opening experience.

Through Honza we made contact with Gertrude, a cousin of my mother, living in Denver. When we first arrived in Denver in 1967, and found an apartment near the seminary, we had no idea there was a relative on the other side of Cheesman Park. We first met her 24 years later. Caroline and I had often walked through the park, and once heard a live concert of *The Sound of Music* there with our three children. We could easily have passed Gertrude without knowing. In addition to Gertrude, my mother's cousin Egon Hochberg, and his wife Hilda, also lived in the USA. They were practicing Jews, involved in some of the Jewish work among the elderly in Los Angeles.

Gertrude was originally from Prague and had lived in an apartment in Old Town Square. One day while she was working in the family business, someone tipped her off: "Don't go back home. The Gestapo are waiting for you."

She took all the money in the till and started her escape, traveling through Italy and eventually heading for South America.

On the ship to Argentina a fellow passenger asked her to take some cash for him. To get into Argentina with this money, they were legally married. Gertrude set up a sewing business and did dressmaking for Eva Perón and other important people. When Argentina became full of ex-Nazis it became difficult for Jews to survive, so she moved to New York and finally retired to Denver. She was in touch with Uncle Beda before he died, and shared with us some of the correspondence she had from him.

In 1991 Caroline and I went back to the Philippines. We made a brief visit to Mindoro but spent most of our two months working with Gospel Literature Outreach in Manila. We stayed a short time with each GLO family, preached at Commonwealth Community Church in the north of the city, and participated in their outreach to Smokey Mountain, which at the time was the capital's largest garbage dump. Many people lived at this landfill site, built little houses, and lived by scrounging through the garbage for things they could recycle.

We also participated in a training program with the Emmaus Church Planting Ministry (ECPM) of the Philippines, and in 1992 at Emmaus Bible School (EBS). One of the students was given the job of helping me with my Tagalog. On the first day he gave me a list of four mistakes I had made that day. Every day the list of mistakes grew longer. At one point he said, "I corrected that mistake yesterday, and you made the same mistake again."

At the end of the course, Caroline asked him how I was doing with my Tagalog.

"*Hindi lamang mali. Pangit ito*," he replied. "It's not only wrong. It's ugly."

We enjoyed attending the classes taught by Dr Dave Johnson. He and a colleague, Dr Ponce de Leon, with help from friends, ran a dental and medical clinic at a church near Mount Pinatubo, northwest of Manila. Mount Pinatubo is a volcano, and had erupted some time before. Along the road, we saw flooded fields and houses. The volcanic ash was used to raise the road surface above the level of the water.

When we arrived at the church, many people were already waiting in line to register with the clinic. An evangelist gave out the literature for our Emmaus correspondence courses and talked to people who were waiting to see the doctor or dentist. Those registered joined one of two lines: one for dental work, another for medical needs.

Before seeing the doctor, the blood pressure and vital signs of patients were checked. Many people had high blood pressure due to eating bagoong. After seeing the doctor they received free medicines.

At noon Rudy Ponce de Leon, the director of the clinic, manned the water pump, and we all washed our hands under running water and had a good Filipino meal with the helpers. After lunch, we continued seeing patients waiting for treatment. By the time they had gone through, many people had completed their first correspondence course.

After the EBS graduation, we visited the town of Hagonoy and saw the fruit of one year of the ministry of the ECPM team members. Twelve months previously, they had just started distributing tracts from house to house when they met a man named Ben at his home. He had been leader of the New People's Army (NPA), a group of Communist insurgents, and everyone was afraid of him.

An illness, possibly a stroke, had left Ben weak and he readily accepted a tract. He listened to the gospel, and the Lord opened his heart. His home became the start of a new assembly. He had ten children. He also had ten brothers with large families. By the time we arrived, several of the family were believers and others were open to the gospel.

Oscar de Leon was the speaker at the kindergarten graduation at Commonwealth Community Church, a church planted by GLO. The kindergarten was a community service aimed at reaching the families of the children for Christ. Kindergarten was not a part of the Philippine school system, but to send a child to a private kindergarten was considered very special. For their graduation, the children were all dressed in white gowns and caps, complete with tassels.

I had the opportunity to visit Oscar and hear his story. He had been a very successful insurance agent, but because he spent more and more time witnessing to people with the gospel, his business declined. His boss asked him to write a plan for getting his business back on track. He wrote a resignation letter instead and began church planting, starting out in faith.

Yet even as we continued to work in the Philippines, I thought of retirement. Was this the place where I would return and stay?

***

The year 1993 was a turning point in our lives and in the history of Czechoslovakia. On January 1, 1993, Czechoslovakia ceased to exist and became two different countries, the Czech Republic and the Slovak

Republic. On January 28, 1993, I had my sixty-second birthday and retired from nursing. Shortly after that, Caroline and I traveled back to the Philippines.

Our plan was to go to the Philippines for a month, then visit northern Thailand, and return to the Philippines for another month. We were also in correspondence with a prominent Czech evangelical named Petr Zeman, based in Brno, and were looking at a ministry in the Czech Republic. But, as the Scottish poet Robert Burns wrote, "The best laid schemes o' mice an' men / Gang aft a-gley [often go awry]."

We took a Philippine Airlines flight to Manila. The next morning we boarded a bus to Batangas, where we caught the ferry-boat to Calapan. We had such a rough trip that on arrival at Calapan Caroline's back was sore, so she stayed at the mission guesthouse to recuperate.

We heard that Werner and Doris Demand were teaching at a conference for indigenous peoples near Paluan. I packed a backpack and set out to join them. At the pier at Abra de Ilog I found a jeep going straight through to Paluan, but when we got to Mamburao there were very few passengers, so the driver went round and round the town looking for passengers to make the trip worthwhile. When we reached Paluan, it was already dark and the jeep driver refused to take me to the bridge where the path to the conference ground started. Instead, he took me to the home of a carpenter, Pablo, a leader in the church.

I was given a warm welcome, well fed, and given a place to sleep. I didn't have a mosquito net with me so I didn't get much sleep that night. Early the next morning, before breakfast, Pablo took me on a tricycle to the bridge about two miles out of town.

Right at that bridge there is a tourist resort with a few treehouses on the banks of the river. I passed the tourist resort and almost immediately saw the fires of the conference. Doris was cooking breakfast and welcomed me to their tree. Each family chose a tree for shelter and slept there. In the center of these family units there was a big tree under which conference meetings were held.

The gathering was primarily a Bible conference, but Werner also taught agriculture. On the steep, sloping hillsides you need to plant rice along the contours of the mountain, and between the rows of rice there need to be little *balanghoy* (cassava) plants to prevent the soil from eroding. While Werner and I met with the adults, Doris had a class with the children. In the evening the children enjoyed swimming in the river while their mothers cooked the dinner.

After the conference, Doris and Werner had business to do in Mamburao, so I went with them. We had a cup of tea at the mission home. I went on to Pambuhan, having made arrangements to meet them on the first jeep in the morning going to Abra de Ilog pier for the morning boat. I got off the bus at the bus stop close to Pambuhan and there were a couple of soldiers with rifles in their arms who stopped me and wanted to know where I was going. When I said I was going to visit Pedro Guilagid, they let me go on my way. Pedro was the village leader of an Iraya church in the west of Mindoro.

I walked up the trail to the village in the hills where Pedro and his huge family lived. This was the place where we had taught the last session of the Mangyan Bible School before we left the Philippines 25 years before. It was great to meet him again, now in his eighties and still very sharp mentally, and very much in charge of the Guilagid clan. There were now about a hundred people in the village descended from Pedro and his wife. It was also good to see how gently he treated his wife, who was obviously suffering from Alzheimer's disease. I joined the family for dinner and was given a place to sleep on the floor.

I was up early in the morning, when the cock crowed, and walked down the road to the jeep stop. It was cool in the early morning air, and I was enjoying the walk down a trail I had walked many times before. It reminded me of the years among the Iraya.

I caught the first jeep in the morning, but Doris and Werner were not on it. I paid the fare and found a seat on the ferry to Batangas. I felt hot. Then I began to shiver. My left leg started to swell. By the time we reached Batangas I was going in and out of consciousness.

A stevedore came onto the boat, saw me, picked up my backpack, took me by the hand, and led me to the boat to Calapan. I lay down on the deck, with my left leg up on top of my backpack. The ship was still waiting for more passengers, so Doris and Werner arrived before it left. Werner told me later that when he saw me, his first thought was, "I'll need to build a box to send his body back to America."

They found a seat close to me for the trip to Calapan. Werner helped me off the ship, and onto a tricycle. Then he helped me walk up to the OMF guesthouse at Bonbon Hill. When I got there, I found out Caroline had recovered from the trip and had gone to visit the village of Bayanan. The guest-home hostess immediately sent someone in the mission's four-wheel-drive vehicle to bring her back to take care of me.

Weak and feverish, I climbed into a bed in a screened room in the same building I had been in many years before. As I was drifting in and out of consciousness, I saw weird pictures in front of me, one after another as if on a revolving roll. I prayed, "Lord, if this is from the devil, please take it away from me." Immediately the pictures stopped, and I have never seen them again.

Caroline took me to a doctor, but he couldn't reach a diagnosis. He wanted to admit me to his private hospital. We asked for oral antibiotics and tried these first, but there seemed to be no response, so I was admitted to the hospital where a nurse started the IV antibiotics.

In the afternoon, Caroline went back to the guesthouse to get some needed supplies for me, including a mosquito net. She had two bags of things she was bringing for me. She pulled out her purse, paid the tricycle driver, and got off the tricycle. She must have dropped her purse in the tricycle, because when she got to my room she had the two bags but no purse, no money, no traveler's checks and no passports.

Caroline immediately put up signs in several parts of town offering a reward for the lost purse. Our provider quickly sent us replacements for the lost traveler's checks. We never saw the cash, but a few days later we got the passports back.

While I was in the hospital, Palay, his daughter, and brother Manuel came to visit me. I had not seen Manuel since the early days of teaching at Badyang in 1959. He was such a chatterbox that he had not been allowed to come to meetings because he disturbed the flow.

A few days later the fever was gone, the swelling of my leg was reduced, and Caroline and I were able to get a seat on our Philippine Airlines flight to Manila. We stayed a few days at the Manila guesthouse and made arrangements for ministry with Gospel Literature Outreach. We took a flight to Legazpi City, and a bus dropped us off right at the church planters' doorstep. We knew one of the men there from the Emmaus Bible School where I had taught a course the previous year.

On Sunday morning we went with the church planters to a new church in another village. It had a roof and a few benches, but no walls. I spoke to the adults, and Caroline had a story for the children. In the afternoon we were back at the church planters' place for their afternoon meeting. After the meeting they opened up the ping-pong table and served a Filipino meal to everyone.

In the following weeks, we spent time with the church planters, enjoyed picnics with them, and went from house to house for Bible studies. Caroline and I traveled together, or when her back bothered her, I traveled alone. I also attended youth fellowships and sports days.

One Sunday morning, I was scheduled to speak at the assembly meeting, but again I wasn't feeling well. I didn't know what was wrong. I returned to the OMF guesthouse and tried to recover from this fever. We finally concluded it was dengue fever. Because I was not recovering, we canceled the trip to northern Thailand and got an earlier flight home to the USA. In the cool atmosphere of our home in Littleton, I soon felt much better.

Our last two visits to the Philippines confirmed that it would be impossible to live there, long term. Instead, my mind returned to the Czech Republic. Yet what could I do there since I could no longer speak Czech? Many people suggested teaching English. Since the 1970s we had had foreign students living with us, and within my own home I had helped with their English as a Second Language (ESL) courses. Had this quiet ministry been a training ground for what was to come?

16

Education for Democracy
1993–1994

I sat in a classroom of American students and scanned the room. I was the oldest by far. Most of these students at the week of orientation in Piešťany, Slovakia, were younger than my own children. Other American students, who had a year or two of experience with Education for Democracy, ran the orientation program.

I had decided to go to the Czech Republic, while Caroline remained home, working on completing the renovations to a house on Acoma Street, Denver, which she had bought as a rental property. I had heard about the program from the Czech Embassy and signed up. Our "teachers" explained the cultural and linguistic shocks they had encountered. They told us not to trust local condoms and to send home urgently for American ones, which didn't concern me. We were told that Czechs do not eat fruit and vegetables, only dumplings, pork, gravy and sauerkraut. The orientation included a good introduction to Czech beer and wine. None of these interested me. I thought only of being close to home, after all these years.

We went for a field trip to an old castle in South Moravia, after which we were introduced to wine tasting in a cellar under a Catholic church. We were served dinner afterwards. When the week of orientation was completed, a chartered bus took us back to Bratislava to catch connections to different towns.

Three of us had been assigned to Labyrint Language School in Trutnov. When we arrived at Labyrint, Joe Kobik, the director of the school, was there to meet us. He offered us several housing options. I moved into an apartment with a lady named Helena Potůčková who was on disability due to asthma and taught some children the basics of English. She wanted to improve her English. I took this option and found that Helena's family had a garden, and there were both fruit and vegetables daily! She was also an avid collector of mushrooms.

At Labyrint there were three classes of day students: advanced, intermediate, and beginners. The school also offered classes to various factories and companies. Joe Kobik scheduled classes for each of us so that we had one day off during the week, because everything in Trutnov closed down at the weekends.

From the first Sunday, I connected with the local churches. Pastor Josef Hudousek at Liberec was scheduled to translate at a meeting of three Baptist churches, gathering together just outside Liberec, and invited me to go with him. I had an opportunity to share my testimony there. Then the pastor of the International Church of Prague gave a message in English. Josef translated it all.

When I was not visiting some other church, I attended the Církev Bratrska church at Trutnov, and I always got a warm welcome from Broňa and Jana Matulik. Broňa came from Brno. He was a professional photographer. He had done his basic theological study and wanted to start a new church in the Brno area, but had been sent to Trutnov. With both of us sent to Trutnov, we had something in common.

Between trips to Liberec, I paid many visits to Brno and stayed with Petr and Daniela Zeman. Through them we had an introduction to many of the Czech assemblies, and I was invited to speak in Prague for a conference. Caroline came to visit me for my birthday, and she was with me at this conference. I learned a lot of things about missionary work in the Czech Republic.

Shortly after settling in at Trutnov, I came home from school and found a letter waiting for me on the kitchen table: "My lungs refused to work. I am here in the hospital to persuade them to work again. Helena."

Apparently, she had been crossing the street behind a bus. The fumes were too much for her, and she collapsed. She was taken to the hospital and was on IV medications for several weeks.

For Christmas, I was introduced to the Czech customs through conversations in class and in actual life. In the town square I saw big water tanks full of live carp, which people bought and kept in their bathtub till December 24. On that day, the carp was hit on the head, cleaned, descaled, and cooked for Christmas dinner. Every part of the

Czech Republic had a different form of nativity scene, but most people did not understand the story behind these figures.

On December 24, I was invited to Broňa and Jana's for lunch. The traditional Christmas dinner of fish soup, and fried carp cutlets with potato salad, was followed by coffee and sweets.

Broňa and I went for a walk while Jana cleaned up and put presents under the tree. When she rang a bell, representing Baby Jesus bringing the presents, we came home and gathered around the Christmas tree. We sang Christmas songs and opened our gifts. I thought about my own family at home. It warmed my heart to think of their laughter around their own Christmas trees.

Between Christmas and New Year, I visited Uncle Jimmie in Edinburgh. I started 1994 back in the country I had been raised in. Uncle Jimmie's daughter Joan, her husband Mark, and their little girl, Deborah, were there. They had recently returned from west Africa where Joan had been diagnosed with multiple sclerosis. Mark was preparing to study for a doctorate to be able to teach at university level. There was a new job waiting for him in Liverpool.

Missing my own family, excitement grew for Caroline's visit. I rented a car and drove to Prague airport to meet her and bring her back to Trutnov. We visited many friends, including a family in Sázava. Olga and her family gave us a warm welcome and asked if, for the next school year, we would be willing to move to Sázava. Olga worked in the glass factory where the firm had 2,000 employees. She was sure there would be lots of opportunities for teaching English. Excitedly, Caroline and I arranged to move there. Joy filled me at the idea that soon Caroline would be serving and ministering with me again.

Meanwhile, Caroline returned to complete the renovations on the Acoma house, and I continued teaching at Trutnov. In May there were some final preparations for the state English exam. After that, many students prepared for university entrance tests, so very few attended classes at Labyrint Language School.

Missing my family, I decided to go home early. The school gave me a farewell, and I visited the police department and asked for permission to leave, and my visa was canceled. I later discovered this was the wrong thing to do, and made the next visa hard to get.

As summer grew to a close, Caroline and I packed our suitcases to the weight limit and returned to the Czech Republic. For the first month, Olga made a place for us in the family chalet on the top of the hill above the glass factory. She sent papers and translations of documents to the police department and the board of education. Unfortunately, Olga translated my MA degree as "Doctor of Theology." The education department sent warnings to the schools that I had only come to spread religious propaganda, and that door closed. Instead, I found myself teaching English at a class at the Economics School in Benešov and also at the Benešov School of Nursing.

For two and a half years in Sázava, I regularly taught at the midweek meeting in the basement of the house where Olga and her family lived. This was a house church. They had received a gift of money from a fellowship in Germany to furnish a room for church meetings in their basement. We also attended a local church as often as possible. In addition we went to Prague for the Sunday afternoon service at the Stodůlky assembly, founded by Petr Vaďura. We took some of our language students and young people with us, and four of them made professions of faith over time.

While in Sázava, family and friends visited. With these visitors we toured the Czech Republic, visiting numerous castles and spending time with some of our Czech friends.

Teaching English as a second language was the door that opened up the Czech Republic to us. Initially, we had to have a contract from a school to be able to get permission to stay past the first month in the country. For the first year in Trutnov, the Labyrint Language School secretary prepared all the papers and made all the arrangements, so I merely had to go to the police office and present the completed documents, have my passport stamped, and collect my little green booklet, "*Prukaz o povolani k pobytu*, permission to stay."

However, every year it seemed more difficult to get this permission, and the cost increased. A contract from a school had to be approved by the Úrad Práce, the employment office. Year after year we went round in circles. The employment office refused to approve the contract because I didn't have permission to stay in the country. The police department dealing with immigration and visas refused to give a visa without a contract. The police always won out.

Then, in the fall of 1999, we discovered that a 1929 law which prohibited dual citizenship had been overturned. Petr Zeman took me to an office in Brno where I asked if I could have dual citizenship. I had to submit an application for a change of name from Thomas Herman Graumann to Tomáš Graumann. I was then issued with a birth certificate. It was a copy of the original in the office of statistics, but a little different from the translated copy I have had since 1939.

A search was started through the archives to determine why I had lost my Czechoslovak citizenship. While we were in Littleton for Christmas 2000, the search was completed and the Czech authorities sent me a registered letter, which was not delivered. When we arrived back in the Czech Republic in January 2001, I got a second letter asking why I had not come to the office to receive my citizenship papers.

The next week, I went back to the relevant government department with Petr Zeman. The officials told me that there was no evidence for losing my citizenship. They gave me a paper stating that I was a citizen, and told me I had to return to Kolín, and at the health insurance office I must ask for an application to be sent to Prague for a *rodne čislo*, my personal number. This process brought me endless frustration.

I went to the insurance office, but was told that I had to go to the town square and ask at the Okresní Úrad, the district office. There an official said, "You live in the village of Nebovidy. You must ask the village mayor to put in the application." The mayor gave me a certificate which stated that I lived in the village, but sent me to the office of pensions and disability insurance. Finally, I found someone who would put in the application.

When I got my personal number, I then needed an identification (ID) card. I completed the application form and handed it in to the authorities.

They said, "Aha! You were a citizen of the city of Brno, so we will send your application to Brno. It will be back in one month."

A month later I asked about it, and again after six weeks and after two months. Eventually I was given a phone number of the office in Brno, and sure enough, it was there waiting for me. I had to go to Brno and get the certificate in person. However, the officials there said, "You are not living in Brno now," so before I was given the ID card they cut off the corner and sent me back to Kolín for a Kolín ID card. After that, it was easy to get my Czech passport.

On the strength of my citizenship, Caroline was able to get a long-term visa. Then the city of Kolín gave me a permit to work as a self-employed teacher of English.

As I held my passport again, I had a renewed sense that I belonged. I had taken an around-the-world journey, but now I was back in my home country once more.

17
Teaching English
1994–2003

For our first month in Sázava, Caroline and I stayed at a friend's chalet, on top of the hill overlooking the glass factory. We became friends with Mr Bubenik, one of the engineers from the factory, and his wife, who was a believer. Bubenik wasn't, but his English was good, and he did some translation at meetings for us anyway. When the couple moved into their retirement home south of Jihlava, we were able to rent their apartment in a high-rise block near the glass factory. It was relatively luxurious: the apartment was fully furnished, and heat was supplied throughout the building. We bought a microwave, and with that addition the kitchen was fully set up. We had a telephone. We bought a TV, video recorder and radio/tape player. This seemed like a dream compared to the Philippines, but after living in the USA it seemed fairly natural to us.

When we got teaching opportunities in Kolín, we were still staying in Sázava but found the cost of gas for travel was high. We found a one-bedroom apartment at Červené Pečky, but soon had to move again. And we found ourselves moving often, sometimes staying with friends. We were excited about the new teaching opportunities, even though at times these living arrangements didn't work out very well.

On workdays, there were several trips a day into and out of Kolín. We usually went by car, but occasionally made use of the bus service. When we first arrived in Nebovidy—a town between Kolín and Sázava— there was a little shop across the street from our apartment. It was very convenient to shop there, and doing so was also a good learning experience as we had to ask for things by name. In the supermarkets we could pick up whatever we wanted and did not need to know the Czech names for all these things.

Gradually we found our feet. I taught pupils in the seventh and ninth grades (aged 11–15) at various secondary schools and private language schools. I also took on private students, both in their homes and in ours. I worked on courses for business people or in factories. Caroline worked hard to get an opportunity to teach an English class in kindergartens.

In the European Union, students were expected to learn at least two foreign languages. The most popular in the Czech Republic were German and English. One Czech teacher told me, "Czechs have a mental block about learning languages. Under the Habsburgs and Nazis they had to learn and speak German. Under the Communists, they had to study Russian. They had a battle to keep their own language, so they do not want to learn additional languages." But English was becoming a common language for business throughout Europe.

During my first year in the Czech Republic, I also started working on getting *Biblical Eldership*, by Alex Strauch, translated into Czech and published. I had first learned about this book in 1981 during our time at Littleton Bible Chapel, where Alex was an elder. Its subject matter is biblical church leadership, and I had used it when teaching a class for men. Also when we visited the Philippines I had been involved in a small-group study of this book. I thought it would really help elders (who were few in number) in Czech churches.

At Easter 1994, at the Easter Conference of Brethren Assemblies, I encountered a good translator, Jan Vopalecky. As a first step I asked Jan to do the translation, even though he was very busy with other projects. He started the translation of *Biblical Eldership* in his spare time, as he was employed by *Ethos*, a magazine published in Switzerland in German and translated into many of the eastern European languages.

After about a year of work on the translation, I was informed that Jan wanted to concentrate on translating German, and the book had been given to Michael Waloschek, a translator in Havířov. Michael also translated a second book, also by Alex Strauch, for me: *The New Testament Deacon*. After years of Communist oppression, Christian literature was now being openly produced in the Czech Republic.

Through friends, I heard many stories of the hardships—and the triumphs—of life under Communist control. One of my friends, Samuel, told us about his mother, Lydia Húšťova. During Communist days she had taught a children's Bible club in her home. Although this was strictly forbidden, she kept an accurate account of who attended each week, what Scripture verses they memorized, and what lessons they were taught. Many of these children from that class were now leaders among the Brethren churches.

During the time of Communist control, representatives of Child Evangelism Fellowship, Biblical Education by Extension, and other Christian organizations used to meet with Samuel and his brother-in-law Pavel, gathering secretly in the forest during the night. They brought Bibles, with other Christian literature, and trained Pavel and Samuel. These two young men became elders of their church. As soon as the Communist regime fell, there was a wide-open door for the gospel. One day Samuel and his friends went to the city square and found someone speaking over a public address system. They asked to borrow the microphone and began to preach the gospel. In addition, *The Jesus Film* was shown all over the country.

Samuel and Pavel taught the lessons they had learned to others until they had 12 trained teachers of children. With help from the Pospíšil brothers, who were well-known Czech athletes, they also started singing and recording children's songs with a Christian theme.

In addition, Samuel and several others from Zlin joined together to form a camp of Gideon International. Samuel arranged to work evening shifts at his factory so that he could visit schools during the day, especially just before Christmas, to distribute New Testaments. One of his helpers would load up his car with boxes of New Testaments while he slept, and the car was ready for the next day's trip.

During the school year of 1998–9 our English classes at Kolín schools seemed to dry up, but Jana Uhlířova from Poděbrady arranged for me to have some classes at the Hotel School where she taught and also at the Gymnázium (high school). She and her husband were hosts of a little Brethren assembly in Poděbrady. This is a spa town, about 12 miles north of Kolín, where people go for the special spa water and luxury treatments—a wealthier town than Kolín. I applied for permission to teach at the Hotel School, and one of the teachers there had a relative in the police department and was able to get my papers approved without difficulty. The Hotel School had two different programs and I taught on both.

During this school year one of my students, Lenka, attended a Christian sports camp and received Jesus as Savior. When she returned from her weekend camp she told her English class, "It was the best vacation I have ever had." When I heard that, I made arrangements for her to meet other young Christians in Poděbrady. She participated in Bible studies and played volleyball with them once a week. She enjoyed being with these young Christians so much that she seldom went home at weekends.

Frequently Lenka also went to the next town, Nymburk, to attend a charismatic church. Near the end of the school year, there was a seminar at this church for children's workers. We went there so we could distribute sets of the lessons which Caroline called the "Egg Story."

A few weeks later, East-West Ministries, which exists to mobilize the body of Christ to evangelize the lost and equip local believers, had a week of evangelism in and around Cvikov. Cvikov is about 62 miles northwest of Kolín, close to the German border. Tom Prochaska came from Texas with a team. We held concerts in several of the towns around Cvikov, and on the streets we talked to people willing to discuss spiritual matters. More than 500 people heard the gospel presentation and prayed to receive Jesus as Savior.

The East-West material included a pamphlet, which asked, "Has anyone ever shown you from the Bible how you can be sure you are going to heaven?"

In a country where most people claim "I don't believe!" it is easy to get a negative response to such a question. The follow-up question was obvious: "May I show you?"

The material was divided into the "bad news"—that everyone sins and cannot get to heaven by his or her own deeds—and the "good news," that God sent his Son as our substitute to take our punishment and pay our debt, and so eternal life is God's free gift to all who will accept it. Most of the time, there were Czech translators available for the Americans. I spoke to some children and with the help of an interpreter went through a children's booklet. Several of them prayed to accept the Lord (I later found out they were the core of the local Baptist church Sunday school!).

One of the translators was very obviously pregnant, and we wondered if she was going to deliver her baby before our week was finished. One afternoon she invited us to her parents' home. It was a beautiful sunny afternoon. They had a picnic ready for us in their garden. It was very pleasant sitting under the shade of the trees, eating beautiful open-faced sandwiches and sipping tea.

First we visited the family's workshop, and all the family members demonstrated how they cut crystal and explained how much work went into a hand-cut crystal vase. Everyone in the group of American visitors was impressed with the difficulty of making the intricate designs. Then we were invited into their sales shop. Almost everyone bought large quantities of these very expensive hand-cut crystals. To make it easier for the shoppers, what they bought was wrapped and mailed to their home address.

On the last day of the mission we took a rented, chartered bus from Cvikov to Liberec. On the top of a hill outside the city there is a uniquely shaped restaurant with a beautiful view of the countryside. The restaurant is located in a circular building with a spire at the top, and serves authentic Czech cuisine. Tom Prochaska's team had lined up this trip as a "thank you" for the interpreters and the local churches, also hoping to involve the new converts with good follow-up.

The bus stopped in the parking lot, and we had to climb up a steep hillside to the restaurant at the top. During the meal, Tom Prochaska acknowledged all the Czech translators, and we thanked them for their help.

From 1999 to 2000 I taught at the private language school at Nymburk and also at the school for nurses. Here I was introduced to the Oxford University course for teaching English, and used their materials from then onward. Because the language school continued lessons till the end of June, I decided to stay and teach till the end of the school year, but sent Caroline home in time to attend the conference of Bridges for Peace, a Jerusalem-based Christian organization supporting Israel and building relationships between Christians and Jews worldwide. Its members also sought to help Jewish people in Israel, and this was our introduction to many Jewish ministries. We had met one of the Bridges for Peace missionaries and heard about their conference at Faith Church, north of Denver. Caroline and I had attended, listened to their talks, read their letters and emails, and prayed for them for years. In this way, Caroline's and my understanding and pride in my family's heritage blossomed and grew.

The weekend after Caroline went home, I visited the Zemans in Brno. Originally I had met Petr Zeman through writing letters. Someone from Operation Mobilization gave me his address, and before going to the Czech Republic we had corresponded. On arriving there, I visited him and his wife Daniela at least once a month, and he introduced me to many of the church leaders in the area. As president of Trans World Radio, an international Christian broadcaster, Petr was well connected and very involved with a number of believers. But one day while in his home I felt unwell, and by morning my left leg was swollen. I knew this was the return of erysipelas, the acute skin infection I had contracted in the Philippines.

Petr Zeman took me to the Military Hospital, which specialized in skin diseases. This was my first experience of being a patient in a locked facility. Because they dealt with skin problems, the nurses were not used to administering IV medications, and they had great difficulty giving me adequate treatment. Petr Zeman insisted on driving me home to Nebovidy, and then to the airport to catch my flight home. Back in the States, I received massive doses of penicillin throughout the summer, but the swelling never went down completely.

From attending the conference of Bridges for Peace, Caroline and I increased our involvement with Jewish ministries and started attending a Messianic fellowship, Congregation Yeshuat Tsion, which met on Saturday mornings at the corner of Holly and Belleview streets in Denver. At this time, we were alternating between living in Littleton and the Czech Republic. I also went to Israel with a Bridges of Peace solidarity mission, during which we visited the town of Ariel, planted some vines on the mountains of Samaria, toured an army camp, visited the work of Christian Friends of Israeli Communities, and participated in a street demonstration in Jerusalem.

During the school year of 2002–3, I taught at Milota Language School in Kutna Hora, a city east of Prague, Caroline taught at a couple of kindergartens, and we had a number of private students, some in Kolín and Kutna Hora, and some in our apartment. We had about 53 lessons a week on our schedule: the days were very full.

One day, I started having chest pains, but all the doctors' offices were closed by the time I finished teaching. One Saturday Petr Trutnovsky, one of my private English students, took me to Kolín Hospital where I saw a cardiologist and was immediately admitted for testing. Petr had previously had heart surgery there, and his was successful. I was then sent by ambulance to a hospital in Prague for a cardiac catheterization. When I was diagnosed with a leaking mitral valve, I told Dr Houra, the cardiologist, that I planned on going to Denver in June.

"If you wait till the summer, you will not be alive," he told me. I was given the choice of surgery in Prague or in Denver.

"Dad, come home," wrote Dan and his wife Wendy in an urgent email to us.

We took the first flight home we could find. Our seats were in the middle of the center section of cabin class. It was hard to get out of my seat. I was not feeling well and didn't look well to Caroline, so when I went to the toilet Caroline spoke to a stewardess. She found us two seats in first class. She talked to the first-class passengers and told them there was a couple coming forward from cabin class because the husband was having chest pains. They gave us a warm welcome to their section of the plane. We were served a first-class meal!

A German doctor, who was on board, took my blood pressure and checked my heart. The stewardess called Paul on the phone, and he was at the airport waiting for me when we arrived at Denver. Paul took me straight to Porter's hospital, and I was immediately put on the schedule for surgery.

Early the next week, I had an eight-hour open-heart surgical operation to replace my mitral valve. Even though the procedure was expensive, we were not too concerned as we had Medicare insurance in the USA, together with Czech general health insurance. We had previously tried to buy medical supplies in the Czech Republic and the price was a hundred percent covered, yet only 20 percent of the total cost was covered in the USA under Medicare. Still, I'm grateful for the good care and coverage we have had.

After several weeks of slow improvement, I was discharged on oxygen to recuperate at Paul's home. I could only walk a few steps outside onto the patio, which was as far as my oxygen tubing would stretch.

A visiting nurse service sent a nurse and a physiotherapist to visit me several times a week, for several weeks. While we were in the USA for this extended time to recover from my open-heart surgery, Caroline had both of her knees replaced. When we returned to the Czech Republic our old school opportunities were gone, but we taught for a year at Hannah Language School.

We had another prolonged stay in the USA, during which Caroline had five eye surgeries. And when we returned after that, we mostly taught private English lessons in our home. Yet, though my body was growing weary, my story and my work wasn't over. In fact, I was soon to discover parts of my story I had never known before.

18

Nicholas Winton and the power of good
1997–2002

All my life I have known that I left Prague with a number tied around my neck in a train full of Jewish children. But I didn't know to whom I owed my life. I didn't know about a man named Nicholas Winton. And it was only after his visit to the Czech Republic that I heard about his meeting with some of the "children" whom he had rescued in 1939.

My jaw dropped open as I watched this story on the evening news. The report showed men and women meeting the Englishman who had made possible their escape from the Nazis' grasp. They were called "Winton Children." All of them had travel papers like I had. And, like me, they had left German-occupied Czechoslovakia with numbers around their necks.

Friends who had also watched the news report called me.

"Were you there?" they asked. "Did you meet Nicholas Winton?"

The man's smile—his face—didn't leave my thoughts. It was to him that I owed my life.

Nicholas Winton paid a second visit to the Czech Republic, and again we weren't aware of it until after the event. I wrote to my cousin, Honza Horský, who worked for Czech TV, and I asked if he could find an address to contact "Nicky" Winton—a term of endearment that so many of his "children" used for him. Honza sent me an address for both Nicky Winton and Matěj Minač, the producer and director of a documentary film about Nicholas Winton. I wrote to both of them.

Decades after getting on that train, I received a partial copy of the list of names of the Winton Children, and I saw my name there. Tears filled my eyes, and my story unfolded before me. I was one of the 669 children rescued by Nicholas Winton.

With both eagerness and thankfulness, I accepted an invitation to Bratislava where Matěj Minač and his film crew were working on Nicky's story. Matěj interviewed me and I answered matter-of-factly. He worked hard to get me to say something more dramatic for his film. Finally, after three hours of watching his efforts, Caroline smiled at him.

"That's all you're going to get," she said. "He isn't a film star."

We were invited to the premiere of the film, titled *The Power of Good*, where we met several of the other Winton Children, including Vera Gissing, a Czech writer. It was thrilling to finally meet Nicholas Winton.

"Thank you," I told him, shaking his hand.

But my simple thanks didn't seem adequate. Nicholas's work had preserved my life and, with God's grace, I too had been able to use it for good.

***

When word got out that I was one of the Winton Children, I received countless opportunities to speak around the Czech Republic. As a result of discovering that Nicholas Winton had rescued me, I had learned a number of things about my story.

In 2001, before moving from Trutnov to Prague, Broňa Matulik arranged a number of evangelistic opportunities in and around Trutnov. He invited several people for special meetings. When I first went to Trutnov, Broňa was pastor of the Church of the Brethren in Trutnov. He had wanted to start a church in Brno, but was sent to Trutnov instead. We immediately developed a friendship. Whenever I didn't have another invitation to speak, I attended his church and was usually invited to his home for lunch. He was the first to invite me to share my testimony, translated into Czech by his wife, and he was the first to write up the initial part of my story, originally printed in his church bulletin.

Slowly more invitations came to speak in schools and churches. Jan Lukl, the pastor of the Czech Brethren church at Kutna Hora, arranged for me to give talks in schools in his town, and he interpreted for me.

When the Matuliks moved to Prague, Broňa became chief editor of their church magazine, *Brana*. This was the publication in which he presented my story, and it was followed by other articles in other Czech magazines.

When I visited the Baptist church in Brno, the people from the Brno Printing Mission interviewed me and prepared a leaflet with my story. They sent a sample to all their regular customers. Soon invitations to speak poured in. Some of these invitations were in Czech and Slovak, so I asked Lenka Vesela, my translator, to answer these letters and schedule my trips and speaking opportunities.

As a result of seeing the credits at the end of the film, Jan Odstracil, the son of the Evangelical pastor who had visited my mother often in Těšany, remembered my name. He contacted me and sent me some interesting papers. In particular, Jan sent me a note my mother had sent him in 1939 when he was ill and couldn't come to my eighth birthday party. He also sent me my mother's last will. Tears filled my eyes as I read this document, and my heart leapt with joy to see one thing she wrote: if she did not return from the concentration camp, she desired that Tony and I should be brought up in an Evangelical family.

"Caroline, listen to this," I said. "In my mother's will she says that she wants me to be trained as a preacher or missionary, and Tony as an engineer."

"Oh, Tom." Caroline's hand touched her face. "That has to mean something. After all those talks with the pastor, maybe she too had come to faith in Christ."

An additional paper helped me to believe this was true. For in those papers was also information about Jan's father's church at Klobouky u Brna. According to church paperwork, my mother had joined the church with her two sons.

Jan also sent other paperwork that was heartbreaking to read, including a list of people sent to Terezin concentration camp near Prague. Mother's and Tony's names were on the list. I had learned that my grandmother had died in Auschwitz, and the story of my father's death was also hard to take. After I was sent away on a train, my father had continued to attempt to pass himself off as non-Jewish. When he was discovered, he tried to run from the Nazis. Then, seeing he couldn't escape, he decided to take his own life, jumping off a high cliff near Brno. My father had initially survived, but later died in the hospital. The story was hard to hear, and it made it clearer to me how desperate the times had been as the Germans continued to round up Jewish people and send them away to concentration camps.

Jan had also sent correspondence between Uncle Beda—Jan Horský—and Jan Odstracil's aunt. With excitement, I took an opportunity to meet Jan. As we talked, I discovered that his father had studied in Edinburgh, and had made the contact for me to go to the Sawyers' home in Scotland.

After I had spoken at Jiří Ortega Gymnázium in Kutna Hora, the school posted my story on its web page. It was then that Dr John Sawyer recognized my name and wrote to the school asking, "Is this the same Tommy Graumann who stayed with my family when I was three years old?"

Even though I was an old man, my past had never seemed closer. Through correspondence, I learned that John Sawyer was a retired professor of Hebrew at Glasgow University and was living in Italy, doing research for books he was writing. Through John, I was also able to correspond with his sister, Claire McGregor. Now I had a connection with both of my young playmates from those few weeks in Dunbar, Scotland, in 1939.

But most amazing, perhaps, was being reunited with Maria of Těšany. Maria had been my friend prior to the Second World War, and her father was our driver and the blacksmith working at our estate. While living in the Czech Republic, Caroline and I had visited Těšany and talked with the village historian. Maria later heard about our visit, and she impressed upon this gentleman that if we were ever to visit again, she should be informed.

When we returned to Těšany with Dan and Wendy, the historian introduced us to Maria, after all those years, and she prepared a dinner for us, complete with plum dumplings.

Then, after the meal, she removed a picture that was hanging on the kitchen wall and took off the back cover. From between the back cover and the front painting, she took out pictures that had been entrusted to her by my mother, including one of me and Tony. We took photos of the pictures, and would have liked to scan them, but Maria wouldn't part with them long enough for us to do so. Over the years, our photos had become very important to her, in memory of my family that used to be. I soon learned that my family's story would become important to many.

Samuel Hust started a ministry in the city of Zlin, at the Tomas Bata University, which was close to his home. I first met Samuel in 1994 at an

Easter conference in Ostrava. He is an elder at the assembly in Zlin and took his inspiration from his mother, who, many years before, had a list of every child who attended her weekly children's meeting, the Scripture verses they memorized, and the Bible passages they studied. Many of those children are now leaders among the Brethren churches. She prayed faithfully for all these boys and girls, and taught them about the Lord all through the years of Communism. Samuel came from a Christian home. His father had been a liaison with the Communist government prior to Petr Zeman, and was bedridden prior to my arrival. Samuel was visited by Child Evangelism Fellowship missionaries who met with him only in the forest, and secretly delivered materials to him. He studied a course on Evangelism, and another on Christian Living. When the youth movement Josiah Venture came to the Czech Republic in 1993, Samuel attended its leadership meeting and has been associated with that ministry ever since.

Samuel invited me to speak at Tomas Bata University and found a lot of interest in my story and the film *The Power of Good*. He asked his neighbors Martin and Martina to make arrangements for me to give some talks in schools over a couple of weeks. Martin and Martina live across the street from Samuel and work with an organization named International Needs.

In March 2008, Caroline and I had a very full two weeks. We stayed with Martin and Martina. They took us into classrooms, and Martin took care of the technology. Four different people translated for me. I spoke at 19 classes in various schools, mostly to eighth- and ninth-grade students (aged 13–14) in primary schools. We usually had lunch with teachers in the school dining rooms and got home for an after-lunch nap.

There were other speaking opportunities in the evenings, including at three church meetings, three clubs, and a library in the next town. This was so successful that Martin and Samuel recommended my program to a Christian project called EXIT Tour. All my life my greatest desire had been to preach the gospel, and now the opportunities continued to unfold before me.

19

EXIT Tour

2008–2009

EXIT Tour began in the Czech Republic as a part of a TV show, *Exit 316*, on Czech television. The TV show was aimed at the younger generation and introduced life values and attitudes supporting healthy lifestyles, and also offered students the chance to solve everyday problems in the light of traditional Christian values.[1]

Originally there were 17 recorded episodes of the *Exit 316* TV show, but their success led to further agreement with the television producers. From 2006 to 2009 there were 80 episodes of the first and second seasons with the name *Exit 316 Mission*. Audiences in the Czech Republic numbered around 200,000 viewers.

The EXIT Tour project was started to create a bridge between the TV show, which addressed thousands of young people, and EXIT Clubs, which worked with young people during the whole year.

The creators of the TV show, Czech television and KAM (Kresťanská Akadémia Mladých, "Christian Youth Academy," also associated with the Josiah Venture movement), decided to broadcast the program on television, and KAM also introduced the idea of holding lectures in schools. The desire was to bring the TV program and what it offers directly to students in their schools. The Czech government had realized there was nothing about Christianity on Czech prime-time TV. To the surprise of many, the authorities asked KAM to produce such a show, which became *Exit 316*. The show concerned a young woman—a ballet dancer—and an angel and a devil, and her choices in life.

So EXIT Tour became the bridge between the TV show and its viewers. The program started at schools in 2008 in the Czech Republic. Just in the

---

1   <http://www.exittour.sk/en/project/>.

first two years, EXIT Tour in the Czech Republic visited 16 towns and 42 schools, and addressed 8,220 students.

After hearing my story, Daniela Rajcova and David Riman visited me at Nebovidy and invited us to join their team. They were coordinators of EXIT Tour, responsible for setting up the program, and making contact with schools and churches in the area they were going to visit. They promised to find a home where Caroline and I could stay and have an after-lunch nap; they would also provide an interpreter and reimburse us for our travel costs. We were very happy to join EXIT Tour.

We visited different towns, and in each town we did a one-day program in three different schools. The event was sponsored by two or three local churches, which set up afternoon events. On at least one evening in each city, the Dismas rock band performed a concert, at which the gospel was explained. With such a full speaking program there was little time for English lessons. But soon my travels expanded beyond the tour, and I received a special invitation.

Out of 669 mostly Jewish children rescued by Nicholas Winton, 22 of us had the opportunity to participate in the seventieth-anniversary "Winton Train." This was a private passenger train that traveled from the Czech Republic to the UK in September 2009 as a tribute to Sir Nicholas, carrying some of the people he had rescued as children and retracing their original journey. Several more Winton Children attended a celebration in the National Museum in Prague the night before the trip started, and others joined us when we arrived in England. My son Dan and my daughter Lynette came from Colorado to join me on the train.

On September 1, 2009, we gathered on platform 1 of the Hlavni Nadrazi, the main train station in Prague, formerly called Wilson Station. The Hottentots musicians played, several people made speeches, and a statue of Nicholas Winton was unveiled. Several of us had the opportunity to sit on the suitcase that was part of the statue, and have our picture taken by friends who gathered to send us off. As we got on the train, I noticed that Milan Michalko, leader of EXIT Tour, was there.

As I looked around at the others, now gray-haired like myself, it struck me that we were gathered to celebrate what we had gained—life—but we couldn't do this without mourning what each of us had lost . . . family.

The train left Prague with two steam engines, one green and the other blue. We all had seating assignments, but we were free to move around the train, talk to other people, and visit the dining cars, piano car, masseur and hairdresser. My daughter Lynette moved from place to place, listening to the stories of other Winton Children on the train. When she returned to our seats, she would relay what she had heard.

"Dad," she said after one of her chats, "I talked to two sisters. There were three sisters originally, and the youngest of them has since passed away. They were in the first train, and their mother had the hardest time sending them away. One of the sisters told me that their youngest sister was just a toddler and their mother wanted her passed back out through the train window. They did this, but then their father forced the mother to put her back through the window onto the train. This happened three times before the train finally pulled away with all three sisters on it."

I nodded as I listened. All of us understood that it was the most unnatural thing a parent could do—to send one's children into the arms of strangers—but it was that very thing that had saved our lives.

Lynette was also amazed at the variety of backgrounds, and how the children now live all around the world. Yet what struck me is how different we would all be if we had stayed.

I noticed the translator of the group, and she appeared to be about my daughter's age. I pulled her aside and asked about her life. Her name was Gabi. She spoke nine languages and had two children. Then I asked about her life under Communism. She shared openly about the oppression—about never feeling safe, never getting to plan one's own future or even trust one's neighbor. She shared about not being able to travel freely, and about the years of emotional darkness and physical hunger. Tears overcame me as I listened to her. So much had been denied to the people of my country during that time, including the gospel. The oppression of Communism was yet another thing I had escaped.

The train was made up of old carriages from the 1930s, including President Masaryk's car. There were first-class and second-class carriages, and even a third-class one with wooden seats. This car was mainly used by reporters for interviews and group pictures of the 22 Winton Children.

The trip was very carefully planned so every detail was taken care of, and we had a very enjoyable trip. A doctor and first-aid team were there in case of emergencies. We also got to know the two tall security guards. My daughter Lynette's husband is a policeman, so she took pictures of all the police officers and police cars as we traveled through Europe, knowing he would be interested to see them. The security guards found her taking a photo of a German police vehicle and asked, "What are you doing?" She explained her reasons, and the men understood. For the rest of the trip we got to know the security guards very well.

Hungarian cooks prepared excellent meals and snacks. The Hottentots Orchestra played the music of the 1930s, and people were invited to come to the piano car and listen or dance.

Frequently along the way, the steam engines needed more water, coal and servicing, so we had stops at several stations. When we crossed the border into Germany at Furth im Wald, the two engines were taken off and a black engine was put in place. Standing on the platform, among many others, was a German gentleman.

"Excuse me, is this black engine a German engine?" I asked him.

He replied in good English, "Yes, and it is my engine. I own this one."

When we arrived at Nuremberg, the platform was all set up for a public meeting. The mayor of Nuremberg and several other people made speeches, welcomed us to Nuremberg, and expressed the desire that another holocaust would never happen.

Volunteers helped the Winton Children take their luggage to the hotel a few yards from the station, where we had dinner and went to bed. Lynette was given a room on the side of the hotel nearest to the station, and slept poorly because she heard all the trains. At this time, Caroline was not able to travel. She had stayed in Littleton because of lung problems. Dan and I were given a room on the other side of the building and slept well.

After an early breakfast at the hotel, we returned to the train and went on toward Köln (Cologne). We stopped at a small town for half an hour just before we arrived at Köln. With several others we walked through the town square. Then the driver of the train invited Dan and Lynette to the engine. When the whistle blew for the train to leave, they jumped out of the engine, ran over some grass, and got into their carriage. Once we had set off, Dan noticed that his mobile phone was missing. He had previously spoken to a German who told him he was responsible for the stations, so this man gave Dan a card allowing him to return to the last station and come back to Köln. Dan went to the spot where he had jumped from the engine, and his mobile phone was right there. He got back to Köln in time for dinner.

In the meantime, some of us went on a tour of Köln. We passed the beautiful cathedral and went by bus to the Documentation Center, which had been the Gestapo headquarters and was now a museum.

We then visited the site of the Jewish Reform-Realgymnasium, where Dr Erich Klibansky taught and was able to save 130 of his students by sending them to the UK in 1938. The Jewish community prepared an excellent dinner for us in the synagogue, and after the rabbi had made a short speech, the Winton Children met in a separate room.

Eva Paddock, a spokesperson for the group, asked us all to share what we had done with the lives that were saved. A number of us had returned to teach English in Czechoslovakia. Tom Berman, poet and scientist, had set up a laboratory in upper Galilee to solve water problems. Several were university professors. After I told my story Eva said, "We don't have time for life histories. Just tell us what you did."

On the third day we went as far as the Hook of Holland, where we had more meetings, with speeches translated by Gabi and others. We got on the ferry and had a good dinner.

All along the way, reporters from all over the world held interviews and took lots of pictures. One little Jewish boy, 11 years old and from Israel, did some excellent interviews, some of which I have seen on the Internet. When we finally arrived in London the reporters got off first, followed by Nicholas Winton's daughter Barbara and her family. Then the 22 Winton Children followed.

Nicholas Winton was sitting on a chair on the platform, waiting for us, his arms outstretched. The station was crowded with reporters, cameras and police. Among the people who made speeches in London were Nicholas Winton, his daughter Barbara, and his grandson Lawrence. One man had done so much, and now the world was hearing his story.

A bus took us from Liverpool Street Station to the Czech Embassy, where there was a fine reception for us. After this we went to the hotel booked for us, while some stayed to watch clips from the upcoming film *Nicky's Family*.

Throughout the trip, my children and I were very conscious of God's timing and guidance. Without planning it, we met several people just at the right time, including Honza Kuklinek and his family near Buckingham Palace. He was head of KAM and was arranging speaking opportunities in Ostrava between EXIT Tour events.

This trip made it possible for me to visit Scotland with Dan and Lynette. Arriving in Connel on the first day of our journey north, we were driving through a construction zone when I told them to pull over. I crossed the street and they followed.

"What is it, Dad?" Lynette asked.

I pointed to a stone cottage. "This is the house where I was raised. Miss Corson lived here. This is where she took me in."

As I stood there, my mind took me through that front door again for the first time, remembering the good people who had laid out a table of food for me and welcomed me with kindness, even though I hadn't understood a word.

Not far away was the secondary school I had attended. We had scheduled some talks, and I spoke in four schools and to a Quaker group.

The second day it was raining sideways, and I turned to my children: "So now you've discovered the real Scotland."

Lynette broke an umbrella as it flipped inside out in the strong wind.

When we visited Dunstaffnage Castle near Oban, we listened to a gentleman who shared a story from long ago about boys who had broken into a room that held swords and other weapons.

A slight smile spread across my face, and I nodded. "Yes, I remember. I was one of those curious boys who got into that room all those years ago."

The man laughed. "So it's you I've been talking about all these years!"

The trip was especially meaningful for me as I realized how close I had been to being trapped within Czechoslovakia. I learned that I had left Prague on the last train that was allowed to leave, in August 1939. I also learned that my brother Tony had been on the train that was not allowed to leave, in September 1939. Tony was sent home instead. Almost all of the children sent home died in concentration camps. Ruth Felmann, who was on the September 1939 train, was sent home and made *aliyah* (immigration) to Israel. Many believe she was the only one of the children from that September train who survived. As we ended our trip, the joy of being rescued was mixed with the ache for those who weren't.

20

Winton Children
2014–2016

From Prague Castle, I received an invitation to attend the honoring of Sir Nicholas Winton on October 28, 2014. Caroline and I were both instructed to wear dark clothing, and friends loaned us appropriate attire. A limousine came to transport us. On arrival at Prague Castle, we were ushered to the appropriate room and there was a seat assigned for me in a row of Winton Children facing the podium.

Crystal chandeliers cast light around the ornate ballroom. A gowned youth choir was arranged in sweeping rows, and a sea of white-haired men and women filled the chairs before them. We had been children the last time many of us had gathered in this city, and now we had come to honor the man who had made it possible for us to be here.

To the left of the podium was seating for children from "Sir Nicholas Winton School," and to the right was seating for family members of Winton Children, with one reserved for Caroline.

A large photo of a smiling Nicholas Winton was erected by the door. At 105 years old, Nicholas sat erect as he was rolled into the room in a wheelchair. His dark suit was perfectly pressed, and his lips pressed into a thin line. I sat too far away to see if tears rimmed his eyes as those in the crowd rose to their feet and applauded him.

Presenting the Order of the White Lion, the Czech president, Miloš Zeman, took what appeared to be a pillow from his hands. He leaned down, extending it toward Nicholas. A look of surprised pleasure filled Nicholas's face.

"It is a great pleasure to confer this award upon two great personalities of the UK," Miloš Zeman said into the microphone, referring to Nicholas Winton and to Winston Churchill, who was honored in the same ceremony. "I am only ashamed it has been awarded so late—but better late than never. Congratulations, Sir Winton. This is our highest honor; we cannot do one higher."

Nicholas spoke into a microphone, his voice trembling:

> I want to thank you all for this enormous expression of thanks for something which happened to me a heck of a long time ago. I am delighted that so many of the children are still about and are here to thank me.
>
> England was the only country at that time willing to accept unaccompanied minors. I thank the British people for making room to accept them, and of course the enormous help given by so many of the Czechs who were at that time doing what they could to fight the Germans and to try to get the children out.[2]

In the back of the room stood a boys' choir in golden robes, and as they lifted their voices to sing, a parade of older children entered, carrying photos—black-and-white images of a time in the distant past. A knot tightened in my throat when I saw my photo among them. Each picture of a child was held beside the man or woman he or she had become. A girl with a photo of me and Tony stood by my side.

After the ceremony, we were ushered into the next room, where we were offered drinks and had an opportunity to speak with others and have pictures taken with Nicky Winton. Not knowing there was a banquet prepared, Caroline and I accepted the invitation of the ushers to go to our waiting limousine, and we went quickly home. By this time Caroline was very tired and probably would not have survived the banquet, which we saw on the TV news that evening.

I was simply thankful I had heard the full story about Nicholas Winton, a young English stockbroker, who came to Prague in 1938. He and his friend, Martin Blake, had planned to go to Switzerland to ski, but Martin called Nicholas from Prague and said that he had been asked to go to Prague and help with the refugee problem. He invited Nicholas to join him.

---

2 <https://www.theguardian.com/world/2014/oct/28/sir-nicholas-winton-british-schindler-order-of-the-white-lion-czech-republic>.

In refugee camps around Prague, the two men found 55,000 Jews. Of these, 20,000 were refugees from the Sudetenland, and 25,000 had come from Germany. Nicholas heard that there were more than 2,000 Jewish children who were in danger of being sent to concentration camps and killed.

Doreen Warrener, representative of the British Committee for Refugees from Czechoslovakia, was glad to give the responsibility for children to Nicholas Winton while she tried to save politically endangered people, such as members of the Christian Democratic Party. He decided something needed to be done for the children, and, as no one else was doing anything for them, he took on this project.

Nicholas Winton contacted many Western countries, and the only countries even willing to help were the UK and Sweden. He worked alongside Eleanor Rathbone, an independent British Member of Parliament, and Rosalind Lee, from the Unitarian Church. He set up an office in Prague, just off Narodni Trida, one of the main avenues in the city. Families brought pictures of their children to this office and filled out application papers to send their children to Britain. When Winton returned to London, Trevor Chadwick took care of the Prague office. Later, Mrs Guthrie Creighton was sent to take Trevor's place in Prague. Winton worked with the British Home Office to prepare travel papers. He pleaded for families in the UK to take in children for the duration of the war or until they were 17 years old.

Nicholas raised £50 sterling for each child. This was a requirement of the British Home Office, which saw the need to have a fund in case the children had to be sent home. He sent pictures of several children to people who were interested, so they could choose a child.

Six hundred and sixty-nine of us acknowledge that it is because of what Nicholas Winton undertook, voluntarily and with very little additional assistance, that we are alive.

On July 1, 2015, Sir Nicholas Winton died quietly in his sleep at the age of 106. Probably more than 5,000 of us owe our lives to him and remember him with grateful thanks. He gave me the opportunity to hear the gospel and believe in the Lord Jesus Christ. This changed the course of my life.

***

My mother loved the theater. How fitting then that my last goodbye to the city of Brno took place in one. Bright lights blared on the stage, and an orchestra played the Czech national anthem. The only other noise on this solemn occasion was the slight shuffling of students rising and then sitting again in their seats. Seven thousand students from Brno filled the place, and I was their honored guest.

It was just a year prior, in 2014, that Caroline and I had completed our final Czech trip together—with much difficulty. She became in need of constant care due to pneumonia. As I traveled with EXIT Tour, Caroline stayed wherever we had accommodation in various towns, and our hosts did an amazing job of caring for us.

In 2015 I had made one solo trip, including speaking for EXIT Tour on alternating weeks, and at meetings in other towns on interim weeks. After being in the Czech Republic for more than 20 years, it was hard to say goodbye to all my friends and co-workers. This place felt like home—in a different way than if I had remained here my whole life—but home all the same.

Now it was October 15, 2015, and the city of Brno had sponsored this final goodbye. After a radio interview, I listened to the volunteer choir and orchestra. When they finished, I stood and shared my story one last time.

My voice filled the space as every student sat quiet, listening.

"I was a small boy of eight when my mother put a number around my neck and placed me on a train to Scotland to save my life."

No matter how many times I tell my story, it never ceases to amaze me.

When I had finished my farewell address, our group passed out New Testaments and tracts at a table where students could pick up literature—one last offering and the greatest gift I could give. I was placed on the train: rescued once. I was offered the gospel of Christ: rescued twice. Twice-rescued child, saved by God under the hardest of circumstances. May my rescue also point to his glory. May it be so to my last breath.

Epilogue
2016–2018

Immediately after the farewell at the theater, we drove to Grandmother's house where the city authorities presented two markers, later set into the sidewalk, indicating that my family had lived there. One marker stated my grandmother's name and the date she died in Auschwitz. The other listed my name and the fact that I was rescued by Nicholas Winton on a Kindertransport.

We then went to Těšany where a similar event took place, sponsored by the mayor of the village. A children's choir sang Czech music, and the cantor from the Jewish community sang the song of thanksgiving for someone's life. In addition, markers for my mother, Tony and me were placed in the sidewalk in front of the mansion. We were told to go to a restaurant in the center of Těšany, and there was a presentation for me from the mayor, including a bottle of Moravian wine and a book about Těšany. The director of South Moravia gave me a wooden box with two bottles of Moravian wine.

The restaurant had some rooms at the back, and the owners offered me one of these for a nap. In the evening, we went back to the mansion, where there was now a meeting hall above a restaurant. Then, after a very full day, we returned to the home of my translator, Lenka Vesela.

At the end of our last meeting with EXIT Tour, the presenters invited me onto the stage, and they lifted me up onto it because there were no steps. They announced that this was my last day with EXIT Tour, and gave me a Czech jacket, a clock, and a stuffed animal in the shape of a mole. "The Little Mole" is a favorite Czech children's story. That was our last presentation with them, but we had some additional opportunities to speak in schools on dates arranged by church leaders. I am very thankful for the EXIT Tour project and for being allowed to contribute to it.

I am also thankful that I was able to attend the memorial for Nicholas Winton in London in 2016. During that time, there were public meetings for the memorial in Guildhall, and we spent some time with Ian Slater, the professional rugby league player, in the town of Rugby—the sport was started at the famous school there. In Rugby I had two opportunities to tell my story. We prayed over every speaking opportunity, asking for the Lord's strength. Looking back on it, I was only able to speak in all these schools in answer to prayer!

Since returning to the USA, I have seen my strength and abilities decline quickly, as health complications developed. I decided to come home when Caroline was fighting pneumonia, and since then her condition has slowly deteriorated. She was helped by Parkinson's medication, but is declining and losing her memory and faculties. I am still trying to participate in Caroline's care, as well as my own now. I expected to look after her but, having fallen and broken an arm and a leg prior to Christmas 2018, I am in need of care too.

I am thankful particularly for my son Dan and daughter-in-law Wendy who have taken such good care of us. And my daughter Lynette who has shown extreme kindness whenever we were facing medical challenges. Also, my son Paul has spent countless hours helping me with this book and encouraging me to share my stories since he was 12 years old. I am equally grateful for the additional years to see my growing family follow Jesus Christ, and we pray for each of them regularly with joy.

In my declining years, I appreciate the support of my family and home church. It is exciting to see young people preparing themselves to become missionaries and serve the Lord regardless of geography. It is thrilling to see the growth and maturation of my family, and a new generation I never expected to live long enough to see! To God be the glory.

Notes from Tricia Goyer and Paul Graumann

A note from Tricia Goyer

My friend Alice joined me to visit my friend Thomas Graumann and his family on a snowy day in November 2018. I had first heard about Thomas when I was on a mission trip to the Czech Republic nine years previously. As I chatted with my Czech friend Gabi, a pastor's wife, she told me about a man who was rescued from Czechoslovakia during the Second World War. It was the first time I had heard about Nicholas Winton and the trains that carried children from death into life. Yet, for these children to survive, their parents had to hand them over into the arms of strangers.

As a mother myself, I can't imagine the pain of those parents. I can't imagine the children's heartache and loss. Years passed, and I couldn't forget Thomas's story, and I asked Gabi for his contact information. After we connected over the phone, a friendship with Thomas was formed, and I spent hours and hours listening to his story. Each time after our chats, I hung up the phone amazed by all that God had done in his life and amazed by Thomas's dedication to the gospel.

Thomas truly embraced God's gift of salvation and dedicated his life to God's service. He surrendered everything to serve the Lord, and the gospel was taken to nations.

Many lives have been touched by Thomas's story, including mine. It brings me a smile to think of the moment when Thomas crosses over into eternity and hears these words: "Well done, good and faithful servant! You have been faithful with a few things; I will put you in charge of many things. Come and share your master's happiness!" (Matthew 25.23).

Thank you, Thomas, for sharing your story with me . . . and with the world.

A note from Paul Graumann

Dad is and was as gentle and quiet as men come, yet his rarely spoken love and motivation were unmistakable. A driven man, he consistently and faithfully found a way to live out his faith in Jesus Christ. The forgiveness of God flowed through him like waves crashing against the rocks on the shore, leaving no room for animosity against anyone. Dad faced daunting challenges with quiet humility, determination and grit seldom equaled. His life is like a spectacle on display of the love of God so great that it demands my allegiance, "my life, my soul, my all." In that, Dad found purpose, meaning and life itself. The love of Christ Jesus our Lord is worth absolutely any cost and does not disappoint. I pray that each of us will also openly receive the Lord's love, and freely share it with everyone in similar gentle humility.